Charles George Harper

The Exeter Road

The Story of the West of England Highway

Charles George Harper

The Exeter Road
The Story of the West of England Highway

ISBN/EAN: 9783744777667

Printed in Europe, USA, Canada, Australia, Japan

Cover: Foto ©ninafisch / pixelio.de

More available books at **www.hansebooks.com**

THE

EXETER ROAD

THE STORY OF
THE WEST OF ENGLAND HIGHWAY

BY CHARLES G. HARPER

AUTHOR OF 'THE BRIGHTON ROAD,' 'THE PORTSMOUTH ROAD,'
'THE DOVER ROAD,' AND 'THE BATH ROAD'

Illustrated by the Author, and from Old-Time
Prints and Pictures

LONDON: CHAPMAN & HALL, LIMITED

1899

THIS, the fifth volume in a series of works purporting to tell the Story of the Great Roads, requires but few forewords; but occasion may be taken to say that perhaps greater care has been exercised than in preceding volumes to collect and put on record those anecdotes and floating traditions of the country, which, the gossip of yesterday, will be the history of to-morrow. These are precisely the things that are neglected by the County Historians at one end of the scale of writers, and the compilers of guide-books at the other; and it is just because this gossip and these local anecdotes are generally passed by and often lost that those which are gathered now will become more valuable as time goes on.

For the inclusion of these hitherto unconsidered trifles much archæology and much purely guide-

book description have been suppressed; nor for this would it seem necessary to appear apologetic, even although local patriotism is a militant force, and resents anything less than a detailed and favourable description of every village, interesting or not.

How militant parochial patriots may be the writer already knows. You may criticise the British Empire and prophesy its downfall if you feel that way inclined, and welcome; but it is the Unpardonable Sin to say that Little Pedlington is anything less than the cleanest, the neatest, and the busiest for its size of all the Sweet Auburns in the land! Has not the writer been promised a bad quarter of an hour by the local press, should he revisit Crayford, after writing of that uncleanly place in the DOVER ROAD? *and have the good folks of Chard still kept the tar and feathers in readiness for him who, daring greatly, presumed to say the place was so quiet that when the stranger appeared in its streets every head was out of doors and windows?*

Point of view is everything. The stranger finds a place charming because everything in it is old, and quiet reigns supreme. Quietude and antiquity, how eminently desirable and delightful when found, he thinks. Not so the dweller in such a spot. He would welcome as a benefactor any one who would rebuild his house in modern style, and would behold with satisfaction the traffic of Cheapside thronging the grass-grown market-place.

No brief is held for such an one in these pages, nor is it likely that the professional antiquary will find in them anything not already known to him. The book, like all its predecessors, and like those that are to follow it, is intended for those who journey down the roads either in person or in imagination, and to their judgment it is left. In conclusion, let me acknowledge the valuable information with regard to Wiltshire afforded me by Cecil Simpson, Esq., than whom no one knows the county better.

CHARLES G. HARPER.

PETERSHAM, SURREY,
October 1899.

List of Illustrations

SEPARATE PLATES

ILLUSTRATIONS IN TEXT

THE ROAD TO EXETER

London (Hyde Park Corner) to—	MILES
Kensington—	
St. Mary Abbots . .	1¼
Addison Road	2½
Hammersmith	3¼
Turnham Green .	5
Brentford—	
Star and Garter	6
Town Hall (cross River Brent and Grand Junction Canal) .	7
Isleworth (Railway Station)	8½
Hounslow (Trinity Church)	9¾
(Cross the Old River, a branch of the River Colne).	
Baber Bridge (cross the New River, a branch of the River Colne)	11¾
East Bedfont . . .	13¼
Staines Bridge (cross River Thames)	16½
Egham . .	18
Virginia Water—	
'Wheatsheaf'	20¾
Sunningdale—	
Railway Station .	22¾
Bagshot—	
'King's Arms'	26¼
'Jolly Farmer'	27¼

	MILES
Camberley	29
York Town	$29\frac{3}{4}$
Blackwater (cross River Blackwater)	$30\frac{3}{4}$
Hartford Bridge .	$35\frac{1}{2}$
Hartley Row	$36\frac{1}{2}$
Hook	40
Water End (for Nately Scures) . .	$41\frac{3}{4}$
Mapledurwell Hatch (cross River Loddon)	43
Basingstoke—	
Market Place	$45\frac{3}{4}$
Worting .	$47\frac{3}{4}$
Clerken Green, and Oakley—	
Railway Station .	$49\frac{3}{4}$
Dean	$51\frac{1}{4}$
Overton . .	$53\frac{1}{2}$
Laverstoke, and Freefolk	$55\frac{1}{2}$
Whitchurch—	
Market House	$56\frac{3}{4}$
Hurstbourne Priors	$58\frac{1}{2}$
Andover—	
Market Place (cross River Anton)	$63\frac{1}{2}$
Little Ann	$65\frac{1}{2}$
Little (or Middle) Wallop (cross River Wallop)	$70\frac{1}{2}$
Lobcombe Corner . . .	$73\frac{3}{4}$
'Winterslow Hut' (cross River Bourne)	75
Salisbury—	
Council House . . .	$81\frac{1}{2}$
West Harnham (cross River Avon) . . .	$82\frac{1}{4}$
Coombe Bissett (cross a branch of the River Avon)	$84\frac{1}{4}$
'Woodyates Inn'	$91\frac{1}{4}$
'Cashmoor Inn'	$96\frac{1}{4}$
Tarrant Hinton (cross River Tarrant)	99
Pimperne .	$101\frac{1}{2}$

	MILES
Blandford—	
Market Place (cross River Stour) . . .	$103\frac{3}{4}$
Winterbourne Whitchurch (cross River Winterbourne)	$108\frac{3}{4}$
Milborne St. Andrews (cross River Milborne)	$111\frac{1}{2}$
Piddletown (cross River Piddle) .	115
Troy Town (cross River Frome) .	$116\frac{1}{4}$
Dorchester—	
Town Hall	120
Winterbourne Abbas (cross River Winterbourne) .	$124\frac{1}{2}$
'Traveller's Rest'	$131\frac{1}{4}$
Bridport—	
Market House (cross River Brit)	$134\frac{1}{2}$
Chideock .	$137\frac{1}{4}$
Morecomblake . .	$138\frac{3}{4}$
Charmouth (cross River Char)	$141\frac{1}{2}$
'Hunter's Lodge Inn'.	145
Axminster—	
Market Place (cross River Axe)	147
(Cross River Yart).	
Kilmington .	$148\frac{3}{4}$
Wilmington (cross River Coly)	153
Honiton	$156\frac{1}{2}$
Fenny Bridges (cross River Otter)	$159\frac{1}{2}$
Fairmile	$161\frac{1}{2}$
Rockbeare . . .	166
Honiton Clyst (cross River Clyst)	$168\frac{1}{4}$
Heavitree	171
Exeter	$172\frac{3}{4}$

I

From Hyde Park Corner, whence it is measured, to the west end of Hounslow town. the Exeter Road is identical with the road to Bath. At that point the ways divide. The right-hand road leads to Bath, by way of Maidenhead; the Exeter Road goes off to the left, through Staines, to Basingstoke, Whitchurch, and Andover; where, at half a mile beyond that town, there is a choice of routes.

The shortest way to Exeter, the 'Queen City of the West,' is by taking the right-hand road at this last point and proceeding thence through Weyhill, Mullen's Pond, Park House, and Amesbury to Deptford Inn, Hindon, Mere, Wincanton, Ilchester, Ilminster, and Honiton. This 'short cut,' which is the hilliest and bleakest of all the bleak and hilly routes to Exeter, is 165 miles, 6 furlongs in length. Another way, not much more than 2¼ miles longer, is by turning to the left at this fork just outside Andover, and going thence to Salisbury, Shaftesbury, Sherborne, Yeovil, Crewkerne, and Chard, to meet the other route at Honiton; at which point, in fact, all routes met. A third way, over $4\frac{1}{2}$ miles longer than the last, instead of leaving Salisbury for Shaftesbury, turns in a more southerly direction, and passing through Blandford, Dorchester, Bridport, and Axminster, reaches Exeter by way of the inevitable Honiton in 172 miles, 6 furlongs.

It is thus, by whichever way you elect to travel, a far cry to Exeter, even in these days; whether you go by rail from Waterloo or Paddington—$171\frac{1}{2}$ and 194 miles respectively, in three hours and three-quarters—or whether you cycle, or drive in a motor car, along the road, when the journey may be accomplished by the stalwart cyclist in a day and a half, and by a swift car in, say, ten hours.

But hush! we are observed, as they say in the melodramas. Let us say fourteen hours, and we shall be safe, and well within the legal limit for motors of twelve miles an hour.

Compare these figures with the very finest performances of that crack coach of the coaching age, the Exeter 'Telegraph,' going by Amesbury and Ilchester, which, with the perfection of equipment, and the finest teams, eventually cut down the time from seventeen to fourteen hours, and was justly considered the wonder of that era; and it will immediately be perceived that the century has well earned its reputation for progress.

It may be well to give a few particulars of the 'Telegraph' here before proceeding. It was started in 1826 by Mrs. Nelson, of the 'Bull,' Aldgate, and originally took seventeen hours between Piccadilly and the 'Half Moon,' Exeter. It left Piccadilly at

5.30 A.M., and arrived at Exeter at 10.30 P.M. Twenty minutes allowed for breakfast at Bagshot, and thirty minutes for dinner at Deptford Inn. The 'Telegraph,' be it said, was put on the road as a rival to the 'Quicksilver' Devonport mail, which, leaving Piccadilly at 8 P.M., arrived at Exeter at 12.34 next day; time, sixteen hours, thirty-four minutes. Going on to Devonport, it arrived at that place at 5.14 P.M., or twenty-one hours, fourteen minutes from London. There were no fewer than twenty-three changes in the 216 miles.

II

But those travellers who, in the early days of coaching, a century and a half ago, desired the safest, speediest, and most comfortable journey to Exeter, went by a very much longer route than any of those already named. They went, in fact, by the Bath Road and thence through Somerset. The Exeter Road beyond Basingstoke was at that period a miserable waggon-track, without a single turnpike; while the road to Bath had, under the management of numerous turnpike-trusts, already become a comparatively fine highway. The Somersetshire squires were also bestirring themselves to improve their roads, despite the strenuous opposition encountered from the peasantry and others on the score of their rights being invaded, and the anticipated ruin of local trade.

A writer of that period, advocating the setting up of turnpikes on the direct road to Exeter, anticipated little trouble in converting that 'waggon-track' into a first-class highway. Four turnpikes, he considered, would suffice very well from Salisbury to Exeter; nor would the improvement of the way over the Downs demand much labour, for the bottom was solid, and one general expense for pickaxe and spade work, for levelling, and for widening at the approaches to the villages would last a long while; experience proving so much, since those portions of the road remained pretty much the same as they had been in the days of Julius Cæsar.

'It may be objected,' continues this reformer, 'that the peasantry will demolish these turnpikes so soon as they are erected, but we will not suppose this is in a well-governed happy state like ours. *Lex non supponet odiosa.* If such terrors were to take place, the great legislative power would lie at the mercy of the rabble. If the mob will not hear reason they must be taught it.

'It may be urged that there are not passengers enough on the Western Road to defray the expenses of erecting these turnpikes. To this I answer by denying the fact; 'tis a road very much frequented, and the natural demands from the West to London and all England on the one part, and from all the eastern counties to Exeter, Plymouth, and Falmouth, etc., on the other are very great, especially in war-time. Besides, were the roads more practicable, the number of travellers would increase, especially of those who make best for towns and inns—namely, such people of fashion and fortune as make various tours in England for pleasure, health, and curiosity. In picturesque counties, like Cornwall and Devon, where the natural curiosities are innumerable, many gentlemen of taste would be fond of making purchases, and spending their fortunes, if with common ease they could readily go to and return from their enchanted castles. Whereas, a family, as things now stand, or a party of gentlemen and ladies, would sooner travel to the South of France and back again than down to Falmouth or the Land's End. And 'tis easier and pleasanter—so that all beyond Sarum or Dorchester is to us *terra incognita*, and the map-makers might, if they pleased, fill the vacuities of Devon and Cornwall with forests, sands, elephants, savages, or what they please. Travellers of every denomination—the wealthy, the man of taste, the idle, the valetudinary would all, if the roads were good, visit once at least the western parts of this island. Whereas, every man and woman that has an hundred superfluous guineas must now turn bird of passage, flit away across the ocean, and expose themselves to the ridicule of the French. Now, what but the goodness of the roads can tempt people to make such expensive and foolish excursions, since, out of fifty knight- and lady-errants, not two, perhaps, can enounce half a dozen French words. Their inns are infinitely worse than ours, the aspect of the country less pleasing; men, manners, customs, laws are no objects with these itinerants, since they can neither speak nor read the language. I have known twelve at a time ready to starve at Paris and lie in the streets, though their purses were well crammed with *louis d'or*. When they wanted to go to bed, they yawned to the chambermaid, or shut their eyes; when hunger attacked, they pointed to their mouths. Even pretty Miss K., and Miss G., realised not the distortion of their labial muscles, but cawed like unfledged birds for food. They paid whatever the French demanded, and were laughed at (not before their faces, indeed) most immeasurably. And yet simpletons of this class spent near £100,000 last year in France.

'But to return. A rich citizen in London, a gentleman of large fortune eastwards, has, perhaps, some very valuable relations or friends in the West. Half a dozen times in his lifetime he hears of their welfare by the post, and once, perhaps, receives a token when the Western curate posts up to town to be initiated into a benefice—and that is all. He thinks no more of visiting them than of traversing the deserts of Nubia, considering them as a sort of separate beings, which might as well be in the moon, or in *Limbo Patrum*.

'I hear the nobility and gentry of Somersetshire have exerted a laudable spirit, and are now actually erecting turnpikes, which will give that fruitful county a better intercourse with its neighbours, and bring an accession of wealth into it; for every wise traveller who goes from London to Exeter, etc. will surely take Bath in his way (as the digression is a mere nothing). At least, all the expensive people with coaches certainly will—and then the supine inhabitants of Wilts and Dorset may repine in vain; for when a road once comes into repute, and persons find a pleasant tour and good usage, they will never return to that which is decried as out of vogue; unless, indeed, they should reason as a Marlborough stage-coachman did when turnpikes were first erected between London and Bath. A new road was planned out, but still my honest man would go round by a miserable waggon-track called "Ramsbury narrow way." One by one, from little to less, he dawdled away all his passengers, and when asked why he was such an obstinate idiot, his answer was (in a grumbling tone) that he was now an aged man: that he relished not new fantasies: that his grandfather and father had driven the aforesaid way before him, and that he would continue in the old track to *his* death, though his four horses only drew a passenger-fly. But the proprietor saw no wit in this: the old *Automedon* "resigned" (in the Court phrase), and was replaced by a youth less conscientious. As a man of honour, I would not conclude without consulting the most solemn-looking waggoner on the road. This proved to be Jack Whipcord, of Blandford. Jack's answer was, that roads had but one object—namely, waggon-driving; that he required but 5 feet width in a lane (which he resolved never to quit), and all the rest might go to the devil. That the gentry ought to stay at home and be damned, and not run gossiping up and down the country. No turnpikes, no improvements of roads for him. The Scripture for him was Jeremiah vi. 16.[1] Thus, finding Jack an

[1] 'Stand ye in the ways, and see, and ask for the old paths, where is the good way, and walk therein, and ye shall find rest for your souls.'

ill-natured brute and a profane country wag, I left him, dissatisfied.'

III

In these pages, which purport to show the old West of England highway as it was in days of old and as it is now, it is not proposed to follow either of the two routes taken by the 'Telegraph' coach or the 'Quicksilver' Devonport mail, by Amesbury or by Shaftesbury, although there will be occasion to mention those smart coaches from time to time. We will take the third route instead, for the reasons that it is practically identical with the course of the *Via Iceniana*, the old Roman military way to Exeter and the West; and, besides being thus in the fullest sense the Exeter Road, is the most picturesque and historic route. This way went in 1826, according to *Cary*, those eminently safe and reliable coaches, the 'Regulator.' in twenty-four hours; the 'Royal Mail,' in twenty-two hours; and the 'Sovereign,' which, as no time is specified, would seem to have journeyed down the road in a haphazard fashion. Of these, the 'Mail' left that famous hostelry, the 'Swan with Two Necks' (known familiarly as the 'Wonderful Bird'), in Lad Lane, City, at 7.30 every evening, and Piccadilly half an hour later, arriving at the 'New London Inn,' Exeter, by six o'clock the following evening.

But even these coaches, which jogged along in so leisurely a fashion, went at a furious and breakneck—

not to say daredevil—pace compared with the time consumed by the stage coach advertised in the *Mercurius Politicus* of 1658 to start from the 'George Inn,' Aldersgate Without, 'every Monday, Wednesday, and Friday. To Salisbury in two days for xxs. To Blandford and Dorchester in two days and a half for xxxs. To Exminster, Nunnington, Axminster, Honiton, and Exeter in four days xls.'

The 'Exeter Fly' of a hundred years later than this, which staggered down to Exeter in three days, under the best conditions, and was the swiftest public conveyance down this road at that time, before the new stages and mails were introduced, had been known, it is credibly reported, to take six.

Palmer's mail coaches, which were started on the Exeter Road in the summer of 1785, rendered all this kind of meandering progress obsolete, except for the poorest class of travellers, who had still for many a long year (indeed, until road travel was killed by the railways) to endure the miseries of a journey in the great hooded luggage waggons of Russell and Company, which, with a team of eight horses, started from Falmouth, and travelling at the rate of three miles an hour, reached London in twelve days. A man on a pony rode beside the team, and with a long whip touched them up when this surprising pace was not maintained. The travellers walked, putting their belongings inside; and when night was come either camped under the ample shelter of the lumbering waggon, or, if it were winter, were accommodated for a trifle in the stable lofts of the inns they halted at. Messrs. Russell and Company were in business for many years as carriers between London and the West, and at a later date—from the '20's until the close of the coaching era—were the proprietors of an intermediate kind of vehicle between the waggon at one extreme and the mail coaches at the other. This was the 'Fly Van,' of which, unlike their more ancient conveyances which set out only three times a week, one started every week-day from either end. This accommodated a class of travellers who did not disdain to travel among the bales and bundles, or to fit themselves in between the knobbly corners of heavy goods, but who would neither walk nor consent to the journey from the Far West occupying the best part of a fortnight. So they paid a trifle more and travelled the distance between Exeter and London in two days, in times when the 'Telegraph,' according to Sir William Knighton, conveyed the aristocratic passenger that distance in seventeen hours. He writes, in his diary, under date of 23rd September 1832, that he started at five o'clock in the morning of that day from Exeter in the 'Telegraph' coach for London. The fare, inside, was £3 : 10s., and, in addition, four coachmen and one guard had to be paid the usual fees which custom had rendered obligatory. They breakfasted at Ilminster and dined at Andover. 'Nothing,' he says, 'can exceed the rapidity with which everything is done. The journey of one hundred and seventy-five miles was accomplished in seventeen hours[1]—breakfast and dinner were so hurried that the cravings of appetite could hardly be

[1] Yes, but the time was cut down to fourteen hours a few years later.

satisfied, and the horses were changed like lightning.' The fare, inside, was therefore practically 5d. a mile, to which must be added at least fifteen shillings in tips to those four coachmen and that guard, bringing the cost of the smartest travelling between London and Exeter up to £4 : 5s. for the single journey; while the fares by waggon and 'Fly Van' would be at the rate of a halfpenny and twopence per mile respectively, something like 7s. 6d. and 29s. 6d.; without, in those cases, the necessity for tipping.

There were, however, more degrees than these in the accommodation and fares for coach travellers. The proper mail coach fare was 4d. a mile, but the mails were not the *ne plus ultra* of speed and comfort even on this road, where the 'Quicksilver' mail ran a famous course. Hence the 5d. a mile by the 'Telegraph.' But it was left to the 'Waggon Coach' to present the greatest disparity of prices and places. This was a vehicle which, under various names, was seen for a considerable period on most of the roads, and can, with a little ingenuity, be looked upon as the precursor of the three classes on railways. There were the first-class 'insides,' the second-class 'outsides,' and those very rank outsiders indeed, the occupants of the shaky wickerwork basket hung on behind, called the 'crate' or the 'rumble-tumble,' who were very often noisily drunken sailors and people who did not mind a little jolting more or less.

Some very fine turns-out were on this road at the end of the '30's. Firstly, there was the 'Royal Mail,' between the 'Swan with Two Necks,' in Lad Lane, and the 'New London Inn,' Exeter, both in those days inns of good solid feeding, with drinking to match. It was of the first-named inn, and of another equally famous, that the poet (who must have been of the fleshly and Bacchic order) wrote :—

> At the Swan with Two Throttles
> I tippled two bottles,
> And bothered the beef at the Bull and the Mouth.

One can readily imagine the sharp-set and shivering traveller, fresh from the perils of the road, 'bothering the beef' with his huge appetite, and tippling the generous liquor (which, of course, was port) with loud appreciative smackings of the lips.

Then there were the 'Sovereign,' the 'Regulator,' and the 'Eclipse,' going by the Blandford and Dorchester route; the 'Prince George,' 'Herald,' 'Pilot,' 'Traveller,' and 'Quicksilver,' by Crewkerne and Yeovil ; and the 'Defiance,' 'Celerity,' and 'Subscription,' by Amesbury and Ilminster ; to leave unnamed the short stages and the bye-road coaches, all helping to swell the traffic in those old days, now utterly forgotten.

IV

A very great authority on coaching — the famous 'Nimrod,' the mainstay of the *Sporting Magazine*— writing in 1836, compares the exquisite perfection to which coaching had attained at that time with the era

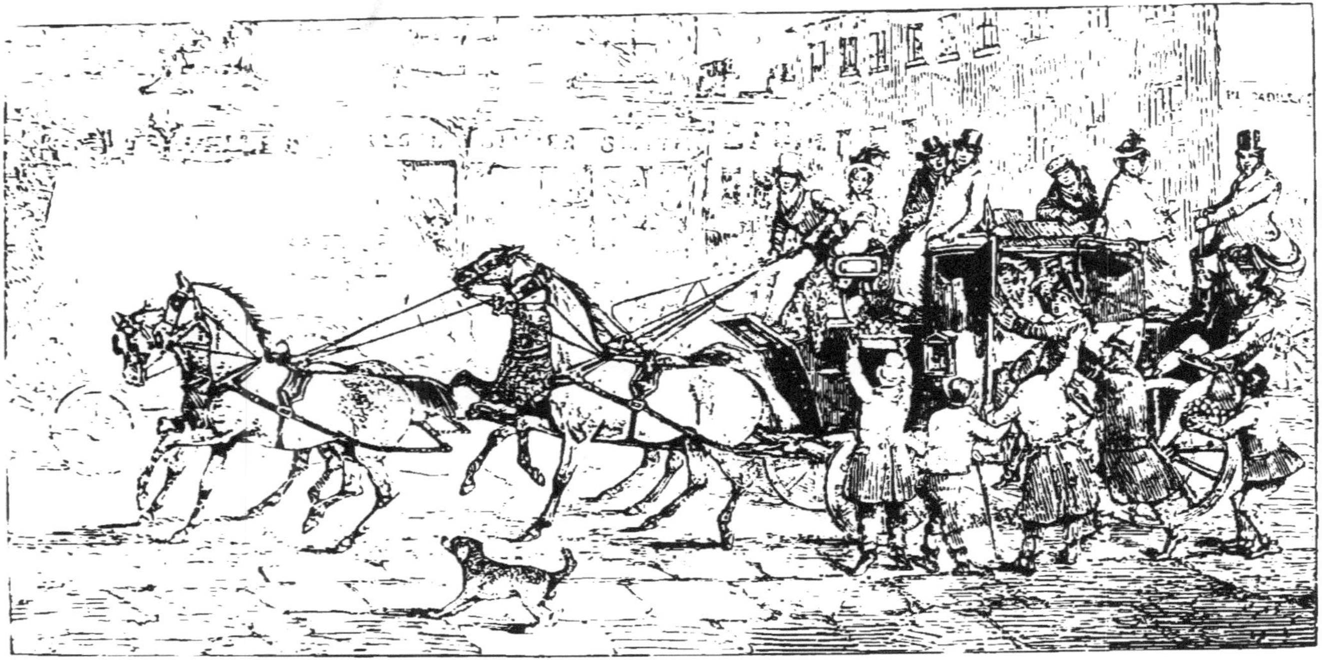

THE 'COMET.'

of the old Exeter 'Fly,' and imagines a kind of Rip Van Winkle old gentleman, who had been a traveller by that crazy conveyance in 1742, waking up and journeying by the 'Comet' of 1836. Rousing from his long sleep, he determines to go by the 'Fly' to Exeter. In the lapse of ninety-four years, however, that vehicle has been relegated to the things that were, and has been utterly forgotten. He waits in Piccadilly. 'What coach, your honour?' asks a ruffianly-looking fellow.

'I wish to go home to Exeter,' replies the old gentleman.

'Just in time, your honour, here she comes—them there gray horses; where's your luggage?'

But the turn-out is so different from those our Rip Van Winkle knew, that he says, 'Don't be in a hurry, that's a gentleman's carriage.'

'It ain't, I tell you,' replies the cad; 'it's the "Comet," and you must be as quick as lightning.' Whereupon, vehemently protesting, the 'cad' and a fellow ruffian shove him forcibly into the coach, despite his anxiety about his luggage.

The old fellow, impressed by the smartness of the Jehu—a smartness to which coachmen had been entire strangers in his time—asks, 'What gentleman is going to drive us?'

'He is no gentleman,' replies the proprietor of the coach, who happens to be sitting at his side; 'but he has been on the "Comet" ever since she started, and is a very steady young man.'

'Pardon my ignorance,' says our ancient, 'from the cleanliness of his person, the neatness of his apparel, and the language he made use of, I mistook him for some enthusiastic bachelor of arts, wishing to become a charioteer after the manner of the illustrious ancients.'

'You must have been long in foreign parts, sir,' observes the proprietor.

Presently they come to Hyde Park Corner. 'What!' exclaims Rip, 'off the stones already?'

'You have never been on the stones,' says a fellow-passenger: 'no stones in London now, sir.'

The old gentleman is engaged upon digesting this information and does not perceive for some time that the coach is a swift one. When he discovers that fact, and mentions it, he is met with the rejoinder, 'We never go fast over this stage.'

So they pass through Brentford. 'Old Brentford still here?' he exclaims; 'a national disgrace!' Then Hounslow, in five minutes under the hour. 'Wonderful travelling, but much too fast to be safe. However, thank Heaven, we are arrived at a good-looking house; and now, waiter, I hope you have got breakf——'

Before the last syllable, however, of the word can be pronounced, the worthy old gentleman's head strikes the back of the coach with a jerk, and the waiter, the inn, and indeed Hounslow itself, disappear in the twinkling of an eye. 'My dear sir,' exclaims he, in surprise, 'you told me we were to change horses at Hounslow. Surely they are not so inhuman as to drive those poor animals another stage at this unmerciful rate!'

'Change horses, sir!' says the proprietor; 'why,

we changed them while you were putting on your spectacles and looking at your watch. Only one minute allowed for it at Hounslow, and it is often done in fifty seconds by those nimble-fingered horse-keepers.'

Then the coach goes fast and faster on the way to Staines. 'We always spring 'em over these six miles,' says the proprietor, in reply to the old gentleman's remark that he really does not like to go so fast. 'Not a pebble as big as a nutmeg on the road, and so even that the equilibrium of a spirit-level could not be disturbed.'

'Bless me!' exclaims the old man, 'what improvements: and the roads!!!'

'They are at perfection, sir,' says the proprietor. 'No horse walks a yard in this coach between London and Exeter—all trotting-ground now.'

'A little *galloping* ground, I fear,' whispers the senior to himself. 'But who has effected all this improvement in your paving?'

'An American of the name of M'Adam,' is the reply; 'but coachmen call him the Colossus of Roads.'

'And pray, my good sir, what sort of horses may you have over the next stage?'

'Oh, sir, no more bo-kickers. It is hilly and severe ground and requires cattle strong and staid. You'll see four as fine horses put to the coach at Staines as ever you saw in a nobleman's carriage in your life.'

'Then we shall have no more galloping—no more springing them as you term it?'

'Not quite so fast over the next stage,' replies the

proprietor; 'but he will make good play over some part of it; for example, when he gets three parts down a hill he lets them loose, and cheats them out of half the one they have to ascend from the bottom of it. In short, they are half-way up it before a horse touches his collar; and we *must* take every advantage with such a fast coach as this, and one that loads so well, or we should never keep our time. We are now to a minute; in fact, the country people no longer look to the *sun* when they want to set their clocks—they look only to the *Comet*.'

Determined to see the changing of the team at the next stage, the old gentleman remarks one of the new horses being led to the coach with a twitch fastened tightly to his nose. 'Holloa, Mr. Horsekeeper!' he says, 'you are going to put an unruly horse in.'—'What! this here '*oss*,' growls the man; 'the quietest hanimal alive, sir.' But the good faith of this pronouncement is somewhat discounted by the coachman's caution, 'Mind what you are about, Bob; don't let him touch the roller-bolt.' Then, 'Let 'em go, and take care of yourselves,' his next remark, seems a little alarming. More alarming still the next happening. The near leader rears right on end, the thoroughbred near-wheeler draws himself back to the extent of his pole-chain, and then, darting forward, gives a sudden start to the coach which nearly dislocates the passengers' necks.

We will not follow every heart-beat of our old friend on this exciting pilgrimage. He quits the coach at Bagshot, congratulating himself on being still safe and sound, and rings the bell for the waiter.

THE 'REGULATOR' ON HARTFORD BRIDGE FLATS.

A well-dressed person appears, whom he takes for the landlord. 'Pray, *sir*,' says he, 'have you any *slow* coach down this road to-day?'—'Why, yes, sir,' replies the waiter. 'We shall have the "Regulator" down in an hour.'

He has breakfast, and at the appointed time the 'Regulator' appears at the door. It is a strong, well-built *drag*, painted chocolate colour, bedaubed all over with gilt letters—a Bull's Head on the doors, a Saracen's Head on the hind boot, and drawn by four strapping horses; but it wants the neatness of the other. The waiter announces that the 'Regulator' is full inside and in front; 'but,' he says, 'you'll have the *gammon-board* all to yourself, and your luggage is in the hind boot.'

'Gammon-board! Pray, what's that? Do you not mean the *basket*?'

'Oh no, sir,' says John, smiling, 'no such a thing on the road now. It's the hind-dickey, as some call it.'

Before ascending to his place, our friend has cast his eye on the team that is about to convey him to Hartford Bridge, the next stage. It consists of four moderate-sized horses, full of power, and still fuller of condition, but with a fair sprinkling of blood; in short, the eye of a judge would have found something about them not very unlike galloping. 'All right!' cries the guard, taking his key-bugle in his hand; and they proceed up the village at a steady pace, to the tune of 'Scots wha hae wi' Wallace bled,' and continue at that pace for the first five miles. The old gentleman again congratulates himself, but prematurely, for they are about to enter upon Hartford Bridge Flats, which have the reputation at this time of being the best five miles for a coach in all England. The coachman now 'springs' his team and they break into a gallop which does those five miles in twenty-three minutes. Half-way across the Flats they meet the returning coachman of the 'Comet,' who has a full view of his quondam passenger—and this is what he saw. He was seated with his back to the horses—his arms extended to each extremity of the guard-irons—his teeth set grim as death—his eyes cast down towards the ground, thinking the less he saw of his danger the better. There was what was called a top-heavy load, perhaps a ton of luggage on the roof, and the horses were of unequal stride; so that the lurches of the 'Regulator' were awful.

Strange to say, the coach arrives safely at Hartford Bridge, but the antiquated passenger has had enough of it, and exclaims that he will *walk* into Devonshire. However, he thinks perhaps he will post down, and asks the waiter, 'What do you charge per mile, posting?'

'One and sixpence, sir.'—'Bless me! just double! Let me see—two hundred miles at two shillings per mile, postboys, turnpikes, etc., £20. This will never do. Have you no coach that does not carry luggage on the top?'—'Oh yes, sir,' replies the waiter; 'we shall have one to-night that is not allowed to carry a bandbox on the roof.'—'That's the one for me; pray, what do you call it?'—'The "Quicksilver" Mail, sir; one of the best out of London.'—'Guarded and

THE 'QUICKSILVER' MAIL: 'STOP, COACHMAN, I HAVE LOST MY HAT AND WIG.'

lighted?'—'Both, sir; blunderbuss and pistols in the sword-case: a lamp each side the coach, and one under the footboard—see to pick up a pin the darkest night of the year.'—'Very fast?'—'Oh no, sir, *just keeps time, and that's all.*'—'That's the coach for me, then,' says our hero.

Unfortunately, the 'Devonport' (commonly called the 'Quicksilver') mail is half a mile faster in the hour than most in England, and is, indeed, one of the miracles of the road. Let us then picture this unfortunate passenger seated in this mail on a pitch-dark night in November. It is true she has no luggage on the roof, nor much to incommode her elsewhere; but she is a mile in the hour faster than the 'Comet,' at least three miles quicker than the 'Regulator,' and she performs more than half her journey by lamplight. It is needless to say, then, our senior soon finds out his mistake; but there is no remedy at hand, for it is dead of night, and all the inns are shut up. The climax of his misfortunes then approaches. He sleeps, and awakes on a stage called the fastest on the journey—it is four miles of ground, and twelve minutes is the time. The old gentleman starts from his seat, dreaming the horses are running away. Determined to see if it is so, although the passengers assure him it is 'all right,' and assure him he will lose his hat if he looks out of window, he *does* look out. The next moment he raises his voice in a stentorian shout: 'Stop, coachman, stop. I have lost my hat and wig!' The coachman hears him not—and in another second the broad wheels of a road waggon have for ever demolished the lost headgear. And so we leave him, hatless, wigless, to his fate.

V

The late Thomas Adolphus Trollope, brother of the better-known Anthony, was never tired of writing voluminously about old times, and what he has to say about the coaches on the Exeter Road is the more interesting and valuable as coming from one who lived and travelled in the times of which he speaks.

The coaches for the South and West of England, he says, started from the 'White Horse Cellars,' Piccadilly, which was one of the fashionable hotels of 1820, the time he treats of.

The 'White Bear,' Piccadilly, he adds, was looked upon with contempt, as being the place whence only the slow coaches started. The mails and stages moved off to the accompaniment of news-vendors pushing the sale of the expensive and heavily taxed newspapers of the period, and the cries of the Jew-boys who sold oranges and cedar pencils on the pavement at sixpence a dozen. Once clear of town, his enthusiasm over the travel of other days finds scope, and he begins: 'What an infinite succession of teams! What an endless vista of ever-changing miles of country! What a delicious sense of belonging to some select and specially important and adventurous section of humanity as we clattered through the streets of quiet little country towns at midnight, or even at three or four o'clock in the morning; ourselves the only souls awake in all the place. What speculations as to the immediate bestowal and occupation of the coachman as he "left you here, sir," in the small hours!'

Then he goes on to give a kind of gossipy history of the smart mails put on the road about 1820.

'A new and accelerated mail-coach service was started under the title of the "Devonport Mail," at that time the fastest in England. Its performances caused a sensation in the coaching world, and it was known in such circles as the "Quicksilver Mail." Its early days had chanced, unfortunately, to be marked by two or three accidents, which naturally gave it an increased celebrity.

'And if it is considered what those men and horses were required to perform, the wonder was, not that the "Quicksilver" should have come to grief two or three times, but rather that it ever made its journey without doing so. What does the railway traveller of the present day, who sees a travelling Post Office and its huge tender, crammed with postal matter, think of the idea of carrying all that mass on one, or perhaps two, coaches? The guard, occupying his solitary post behind the coach on the top of the receptacle called, with reference to the constructions of still earlier days, the *hinder*-boot, sat on a little seat made for one, with his pistol and blunderbuss in a box in front of him. And the original notion of those who first planned the modern mail coach was that the bags containing the letters should be carried in the *hinder*-boot. The fore-boot, beneath the driver's box, was considered to be appropriated to the baggage of the three outside and four inside passengers, which was the *Mail's* entire complement. One of the outsiders shared the box with the driver, and two occupied the seat on the roof behind him, their backs to the horses, and facing the guard, who had a seat all to himself. The accommodation provided for these two was not of a very comfortable description. They were not, indeed, crowded, as the four who occupied a similar position on another coach often were; but they had a mere board to sit on, whereas the seats on the roof of an ordinary stage coach were provided with cushions. The fares by the mail were nearly always somewhat higher than those by even equally fast, or, in some cases, faster, coaches; and it seems unreasonable, therefore, that the accommodation should have been inferior. I can only suppose that the patrons of the mail were understood to be compensated for its material imperfections by the superior dignity of their position. The *box*-seat, however, was well cushioned.

But if the despatches, which it was the mail's business to carry, could once upon a time be contained in the hinder-boot, such soon ceased to be the case. The bulk of postal matter which had to be carried was constantly and rapidly increasing, and often as many as nine enormous sacks, which were as long as the coach was broad, were heaped upon the roof. The huge heap, three or four tiers high, was piled to a height which prevented the guard, even when standing, from seeing or communicating with the coachman. If to these considerations the reader will add the consideration of the Devon and Somerset roads, over which this top-heavy load had to be carried at twelve miles an hour, it will not seem strange that accidents should have occurred. Not that the roads were bad. They, thanks to M'Adam, were good, hard, and smooth, but the hills were numerous and steep.

'The whole of the service was well done and admirable, and the drivers of such a coach were masters of their profession. Work hard, but remuneration good. There were fewer passengers by the mail to "remember" the coachman, but it was more uniformly full, and somewhat more was expected from a traveller by the mail. It was a splendid thing to see the beautiful teams going over their short stage at twelve miles an hour. None but good cattle in first-rate condition could do the work. A saying of old Mrs. Mountain, for many years the well-known proprietress of one of the large coaching inns in London, used to be quoted as having been addressed by her to one of her drivers: "You find whip-cord, John, and I'll find oats." And, as it used to be said, the measure of the corn supplied to a coach-horse was—his stomach!

'It was a pretty sight to see the changing of the horses. There stood the fresh team, two on the off side, two on the near side, and the coach was drawn up with the utmost exactitude between them. Four ostlers jump to the splinter-bars and loose the traces: the reins have already been thrown down. The driver retains his seat, and, within the minute (more than once, within fifty seconds by the watch) the coach is again on its onward journey.

'Then how welcome was breakfast at an excellent old-world country inn—twenty minutes allowed. The hot tea, after your night's drive, the fresh cream, butter, eggs, hot toast, and cold beef, and then, with your cigar alight, back to the box and off again.

'I once witnessed on that road—not quite *that* road, for the "Quicksilver" took a somewhat different line—the stage of four miles between Ilchester and Ilminster done in *twenty* minutes, and a trace broken and mended on the road. The mending was effected by the guard almost before the coach stopped. It is a level bit of road, four miles only for the entire stage, and was performed at a full gallop. That was done by a coach called the "Telegraph," started some years after the "Quicksilver," to do the distance between Exeter and London in one day. We started at 5 A.M. from Exeter and reached London between 9 and 10 that night, with time for breakfast and dinner on the road. I think the performance of the Exeter "Telegraph" was the *ne plus ultra* of coach-travelling. One man drove fifty miles, and then meeting the other coach on the road, changed from one box to another and drove the fifty miles back. It was tremendously hard work. "Not much work for the whip arm?" I asked a coachman. "Not much, sir; but just put your hand on my left arm." The muscle was swollen to its utmost, and as hard as iron. Many people who have not tried it think it easier work to drive such a coach and such a team as this than to have to flog a dull team up to eight miles an hour.'

Thomas Adolphus Trollope's reminiscences may be

fitly supplemented by those of Moses James Nobbs, who died in June 1897, at the age of eighty years, and was one of the last of the mail-guards on the Exeter Road. To say that he was actually *the* last would be rash, for coachmen, postboys, and guards were a long-lived race, and it would not be at all surprising to learn that some ancient veterans still survive. Nobbs entered the service of the Post Office in 1836, and was transferred from the Bristol and Portsmouth to the London, Yeovil, and Exeter Mail in 1837.

Retiring at the close of 1891, he therefore saw fifty-five years' service, and vividly recollected the time when the mails were conveyed in bags secured on the roof of the coach. At Christmas-time the load was always heavy: but although the correspondence of that season sometimes severely strained the capacity of the vehicle, it is not recorded that the mail had to be duplicated, as had to be done sometimes in after years when railways had superseded coaches.

When the Great Western Railway was opened through to Exeter in 1844 and the last mail coach on this route had been withdrawn, Nobbs was given the superintendence of the receiving and despatching of the mails from Paddington, and often spoke of the extraordinary growth of the Post Office business during the railway era. At one Christmas-tide he despatched from Paddington in a single day no less than twenty tons of letters and parcels.

He had not been without his adventures. 'We had a very sad accident,' he says, 'with that mail on one occasion, between Whitchurch and Andover. The coach used to start from Piccadilly, where all the passengers and baggage were taken up. On this occasion the bags were brought up in a cart, as usual, and we were off in a few seconds. My coachman had been having a drinking bout with a friend that day, and when we had got a few miles on the road, I discovered that he was the worse for drink and that it was not safe for him to drive. So when we reached Hounslow I made him get off the box-seat; and after securing the mail-bags and putting him in my seat and strapping him in, I took the ribbons. At Whitchurch the coachman unstrapped himself and exchanged places with me, but we had not proceeded more than three miles when, the coach giving a jolt over a heap of stones, he fell between the horses, and the wheels of the coach ran over him, killing him on the spot. The horses, having no driver, broke into a full gallop, so, as there was no front passenger, I climbed over the roof, to gather up the reins, when I found that they had fallen among the horses' feet and were trodden to bits. Returning over the roof, I missed my hold and fell into the road, but fortunately with no worse accident than some bruises and a sprained ankle. The horses kept on till they reached Andover, where they pulled up at the usual spot. Strange to say, no damage was done to the coach, though there was a very steep hill to go down. The "Old Exeter Mail," which came behind our coach, found the body of my coachman on the road, and, a mile farther, picked me up.'

VI

Suppose, instead of taking one of the fast mails to Exeter, and journeying straight away, we book a seat in one of the 'short stages' which were the only popular means of being conveyed between London and the suburbs in the days before railways, omnibuses, and tramways existed. We will take the stage to Brentford, because that is on our way.

What year shall we imagine it to be? Say 1837, because that date marks the accession of Her Majesty and the opening of the great Victorian Era, in which everything except human nature (which is still pretty much what it used to be) has been turned inside out, altered, and 'improved.'

If, in the year 1837, we wished to reach Brentford and could not afford to hire a trap or carriage, practically the only way, other than walking the seven miles, would have been to take the stage; and as these stages, starting from the City or the Strand, were comparatively few, it was always advisable to go down to the starting-places and secure a seat, rather than to chance finding one vacant at Hyde Park Corner.

'How we hate the Putney and Brentford stages that draw up in a line in Piccadilly, after the mails are gone,' says Hazlitt, writing of the romance of the Mail Coach. Well, it may be that their five or ten mile journeys afforded no hold for the imagination, compared with the dashing 'Quicksilver' and the lightning 'Telegraph' to Exeter; but what on earth the Londoner of modest means who desired to travel to Putney or to Brentford would in those pre-omnibus times have done without those stages it is impossible to conceive. We, in these days, might just as well find romance in the majesty of the beautiful Great Western Express locomotives that speed between Paddington and Penzance, and then turn to the omnibuses that run to Hammersmith, and say, 'How we hate the 'buses!'

All these suburban stages started from public-houses. There were quite a number which went to Brentford and on to Hounslow, and they set out from such forgotten houses as the 'New Inn,' Old Bailey; the 'Goose and Gridiron,' St. Paul's Churchyard; the 'Old Bell,' Holborn; the 'Gloucester Coffee House,' Piccadilly; the 'White Hart,' 'Red Lion,' and 'Spotted Dog,' Strand; and the 'Bolt-in-Tun,' Fleet Street. It is to be feared that those stages were not 'Swiftsures,' 'Hirondelles,' or 'Lightnings.' Nor, indeed, were 'popular prices' known in those days. Concessions had been made in this direction, it is true, some seven years before, when the man with the extraordinary name—Mr. Shillibeer—introduced the first omnibus, which ran between the 'Yorkshire Stingo,' in the New Road, Marylebone, and the City: and the very name 'omnibus' was originally intended as a kind of finger-post to point out the intended popularity of the new conveyance, but as the fare to the City was one shilling, it may readily be supposed that Bill Mortarmixer, Tom Tenon, and the whole of

THE WEST COUNTRY MAILS STARTING FROM THE GLOUCESTER COFFEE HOUSE, PICCADILLY (AFTER JAMES POLLARD).

their artisan brethren, who did not in those times aspire to one-and-twopence per hour, preferred to walk. For the same reason, they were only the comparatively affluent who could afford the eighteenpenny fare, or the two-hours journey, to Brentford by the 'stage.'

Let us suppose ourselves to be of that fortunate company, and, paying our one-and-sixpence, set out from the 'Goose and Gridiron.'

That old-fashioned hostelry, which stood modestly back from the roadway on the north side of St. Paul's Churchyard, was, unhappily, demolished in 1894, after a good deal more than two centuries' record for good cheer. It was originally the 'Swan and Harp,' but some irreverent wag, probably as far back as the building of the house in Wren's time, found the other name for it, and the effigies of the goose and the gridiron remained even to our own time.

This year of our imaginary journey affords a strange contrast with the appearance the streets will possess some sixty years later. Ludgate Hill, in 1837 an exceedingly narrow thoroughfare, paved with rough granite setts, will in the last decade of the century present a very different aspect. Instead of the dingy brick warehouses there will be handsome premises of some architectural pretensions, and the Hill will be considerably widened. The setts will have disappeared, to be replaced by wood pavement, and the traffic will have increased tenfold; until, in fact, it has become a continuous stream. There will be strange vehicles, too, unknown in 1837, omnibuses, hansom-cabs, and motor cars, and where Ludgate Hill joins Fleet Street there will be a Circus and an obstructive railway-bridge.

We proceed in leisurely fashion down Ludgate Hill, and halt for passengers and parcels at the 'Bolt-in-Tun,' Fleet Street, which is now a railway receiving office. Thence by slow degrees, calling at the 'Red Lion,' 'Spotted Dog,' and the 'White Hart,' we eventually reach the 'Gloucester Coffee House,' Piccadilly, re-built many years ago, and now the 'Berkeley Hotel.' Beyond this point, progress is fortunately speedier, and we reach Hyde Park Corner in, comparatively speaking, the twinkling of an eye. Hyde Park Corner in 1837, this year of the Queen's accession, has begun to feel the great changes that are presently to alter London so marvellously. We have among our fellow-travellers by the stage an old gentleman, a Cobbett-like person, who wears a rustic, semi-farmer kind of appearance, and recollects many improvements here; who can 'mind the time, look you,' when the turnpike-gate (which was removed in 1825) stood at the corner; when St. George's Hospital was a private mansion, the residence of Lord Lanesborough; and when the road leading past it to Pimlico was quite wild country, as in the picture on page 43, where sportsmen shot snipe in those marshes that were in future years

'AN OLD GENTLEMAN, A COBBETT-LIKE PERSON.'

THE DUKE OF WELLINGTON'S STATUE.

to become the site of Belgrave Square and other aristocratic quarters.

At this spot Mr. Decimus Burton had already built the great Triumphal Arch forming the entrance to Constitution Hill, together with the Classic Screen at Hyde Park Corner. The Screen was built in 1828, and the Arch, which is a copy of the Arch of Titus at Rome, in 1832. Already, in 1820, Apsley House had become the residence of the Iron Duke, but it was not until 1846 that what Thackeray justly names 'the hideous equestrian monster' was placed on the summit of that Arch, opposite the Duke's windows. Here is an illustration of it, before it was hoisted up to that height. Beside it you see the Duke himself, in his characteristic white trousers, in company with several weirdly dressed persons. Again, over page, may be seen the Arch, with the statue on it, and the neighbourhood vastly changed from the appearance it wears in the picture of the 'North-East Prospect of St. George's Hospital.' Instead of the great hooded waggons starting for the West Country, the road is occupied with very crowded traffic, and among the vehicles may be noticed two omnibuses, one going to Chelsea, the other (for this is the year 1851) to the Exhibition,—the first exhibition that ever was. If, ladies and gentlemen, you will be pleased to look at those omnibuses, you will see that they have neither knifeboards nor seats on the roof, and that passengers are squatting up there in the most supremely uncomfortable, not to say dangerous, positions. Also, in those dark ages of London locomotion, the ascent to that uncomfortable roof was of itself perilous, for no

THE WELLINGTON ARCH AND HYDE PARK CORNER, 1851.

ST. GEORGE'S HOSPITAL, AND THE ROAD TO PIMLICO, 1780.

one had as yet dreamed of the staircase. Other curious points will be noticed by the observant, and among them the fact that 'buses then had doors. The present historian vividly recollects a door being part of the equipment of every 'bus, and of the full-flavoured odour of what Mr. W. S. Gilbert calls 'damp straw and squalid hay' which assailed the nostrils of the 'insides' when that door was shut; but in what particular year did the door vanish altogether? Alas! the straw, with the door, is gone for evermore, and passengers no longer lose their small change in it to the great gain of the conductor, who, by the way, used to be called 'the cad,' even although he commonly wore a 'top hat' and a frock coat, as per the picture. The word 'cad' has since then acquired a much more offensive meaning, and if you addressed a conductor by that name nowadays, he would probably express a desire to punch your head.

The hideous statue of the Duke and his charger 'Copenhagen,' which the French said 'avenged Waterloo,' was removed to Aldershot in 1884, when the alterations were made at Hyde Park Corner.

VII

And now we come to the first toll-gate, which, removed to this spot in 1825, opposite where the Alexandra Hotel now stands, stood here until 1854.

There were many troublesome survivals in 1837 which have long since been swept away. Toll-gates,

KNIGHTSBRIDGE TOLL-GATE, 1854.

for instance. The toll or turnpike gate of sixty, fifty, forty years ago was a very real grievance, both on country roads and in London itself, or in those districts which we now call London. Many people objected to pay toll then, and a favourite amusement of the young bloods was fighting the pikeman for his halfpenny, his penny, or his sixpence, as the case might be. Sometimes the pikeman won, sometimes those gay young sparks; and the pikeman always took those terrific encounters as part of the day's work, and never summoned those sportsmen for assault and battery. In fact, they were such sporting times that, whether the pikeman or the Corinthian youth won, the latter would probably chuck his antagonist a substantial coin of the realm, whereupon the pikeman would say that 'his honour was a gemman,' and exeunt severally to purchase beef-steaks for the reduction of black eyes.

THE PIKEMAN.

The present generation has, of course, never seen a pikeman. He wore a tall black glazed hat and corduroy breeches, with white stockings. But the most distinctive part of his costume was his white linen apron. No one knows why he wore an apron; neither did he, and the reason of it must now needs be lost in the mists of history, because the last pikeman, whom otherwise we might have asked, is dead, and gone to Hades, where he probably is still going through a series of shadowy encounters beside the shores of the Styx with the ghosts of the Toms and Jerrys of long ago, and offering to fight Charon for the price of his ferry across the stream.

But here we are at rural Knightsbridge, in 1837 as quiet a spot as you could find round London, with scattered cottages of the rustic, rose-embowered kind. Knightsbridge Green *was* a green in those days, and not, as it is now, a squalid paved court. Then, and for many years afterwards, the soldiers from the neighbouring barracks would walk with the nurse-maids in the country lanes, and take tea in the tea-gardens which stood away behind the highroad and were a feature of Brompton. Where are those tea-gardens now, and where the toll-gate that barred the road by the barracks? Gone, my friends; swept away like the gossamer threads of the spiders that spun webs in the arbours of those gardens and dropped in the nursemaids' tea and the soldiers' beer. Those soldiers and those nursemaids are gone too, else it would be a pleasing, a curious, and an instructive thing to take them, tottering in their old age, by the hand and say: 'Here, my gallant warrior of eighty years or so,' and 'Here, my pretty maiden of four-score, is Knightsbridge, the self-same Knightsbridge you knew, but with some new, and somewhat larger, buildings.' They would be as strangers in a strange land, and, dazed by the din of the thronging traffic amid the sky-scraping buildings, beg to be taken

KNIGHTSBRIDGE BARRACKS TOLL-GATE.

E

away. But to bring back the policeman of that era, if that were possible, and set him to control this traffic, would be more instructive still. When the last years of the coaching age along this road were still running their course, 'Robert,' the 'Peeler,' or the 'New Police,' as he was variously named, had an easy time of it here. Not so his successors, who have to deal with an almost continual block, all day long and every day.

THE 'NEW POLICE.'

The 'New Police' were a novel body of men in the early years of the reign, having been introduced in 1829 by Sir Robert Peel. Hence the brilliant appropriateness of those nicknames. There still, however, lingered in various parts of the Metropolis that ancient institution, the Watchman, who patrolled the streets at night and announced the hours in a curious sing-song voice with remarks upon the state of the weather added. Those who sat up late were familiar with the chant: 'Twelve o'clock, and a stormy night!' and found comfort in the companionship of that voice.

The watchmen, although scarce anyone now living can have seen one of those many-caped, tottering old fellows, seem strangely familiar to us. That is because we have read so much about them in the exploits of Tom and Jerry, the Corinthian youth of the glorious days of George the Fourth, when the most popular forms of sport were knocker-wrenching, bilking a pikeman, and thrashing a Charley. A

'Charley' was, of course, a watchman. The thrashing of a 'Charley' was not an heroic pursuit, but (or, rather, therefore) it was extremely popular. They were generally old men, and not capable of very serious reprisals upon the gangs of muscular youths who thumped, whacked, larrupped, and beat them unmercifully, and overturned their watch-boxes on to them, so that those poor old men were imprisoned until some Samaritan came by and released them. No one ever attempted that sort of thing with the 'New Police,' who were not old and decrepit men, but tall, lusty, upstanding fellows. Perhaps that was why the 'New Police' were so violently objected to, although the ostensible grounds of objection were founded on the supposition that the continental system of a semi-military *gendarmerie* was intended. The authorities were therefore at great pains to keep the police a strictly citizen force, and although a uniform was, of course, necessary, one as nearly as possible like civilian dress was chosen. The present uniform of the police, and the police themselves, if they had then worn a helmet, would have been howled out of existence by the violent Radicals and Chartists who troubled the early years of the Queen's reign. They did not, therefore, wear a helmet at all, but a tall glazed hat of the chimney-pot kind. A swallow-tailed coat, tightly buttoned up, with a belt round the waist, a stiff stock under the chin, and trousers of white duck gave him, altogether, a very respectable and citizen-like aspect. It has been left to later years to alter this uniform.

VIII

But we must not forget that we are travelling to Brentford sixty-two years ago. Let us, therefore, whip up the horses, and, passing the first milestone at the corner of the lane which a future generation to that of 1837 is to know by the name of the Exhibition Road, hurry on to Kensington.

TOMMY ATKINS, 1838.

Kensington in this year of the accession of Her Majesty Queen Victoria is having an unusual amount of attention paid to it. Every one is bursting with loyalty towards the girl of eighteen suddenly called upon to rule over the nation, and crowds throng the old-fashioned High Street of Kensington at the end by Palace Green, eager to see Her Majesty drive forth from Kensington Palace. They are kept at a respectful distance by a sentry in a dress which succeeding generations will think absurd. White trousers, coatee, stiff stock, rigid cross-belts, and a shako like the upper part of the funnel of a penny steamer were whimsical things to go a-soldiering in, but the Tommy Atkins of that time had no other or easier kind of uniform, and it will be left for the Crimean War, seventeen years later, to prove the folly of it.

The palace is well guarded, for the Government, for their part, have not yet learned to trust the people; nor, indeed, are the people at this time altogether to be trusted. The long era of the Georges did not breed loyalty, and for William the Fourth, just dead, the people had an amused contempt. They called him 'Silly Billy.' At this time, also, aristocracy drew its skirts daintily from any possible contact with

OLD KENSINGTON CHURCH.

the lower herd. Alas! poor lower herd, and still more, alas! for aristocracy.

Our fellow-traveller in the Brentford stage has a friend with him, and, as we jolt from Kensington Gore into the High Street, points out the palace, and tells how William the Third and Queen Mary lived and died there, amid William's stolid Hollanders. He tells a story which he heard from his grandfather, of how Dr. Radcliffe, called in to look at the King's dropsical ankles, said, when asked what he thought of them, 'Why, truly. I would not have your Majesty's two legs for your three kingdoms.' He tells the friend that the King procured a more courtly and less blunt medical adviser: and we can well believe it. More stories beguile the way: how Queen Anne and Prince George of Denmark ended here in the fulness of time: how their successor, George the First, furious with Sir Robert Walpole, with his queen, with the servants, and anything and everything, used to tear off his wig and jump on it, in transports of rage. How he would gaze up at the vane on the clock-tower entrance to the palace (which we can just glimpse as we pass), anxious for favouring winds to waft his ships to England with despatches from his beloved Hanover, and how he died suddenly at breakfast one morning after being disappointed in those breezes.

These are hearsay stories. Our friend, however, has reminiscences of his own, and can recollect the Princess Caroline, the eccentric wife of the Prince Regent, living at the palace between the years 1810 and 1814—'a red-faced huzzy, sir, with yellow towzled hair, all spangles and scarlet cloak, like a play-actress, making Haroun-al-Raschid visits among the people, and bothering the house-agents in the neighbourhood for houses to let.' The old gentleman who says this is a Radical, and, like all of that political creed, likes to see Royalty 'behaving as sich, and not like common people such as you an' me.' Whereupon another passenger in the stage, on whom the speaker's eye has fallen, audibly objects to being called, or thought, or included among common persons: so that relations among the 'insides' are strained, and so continue, past Kensington Church, a very decrepit and nondescript kind of building; past the Charity School, the Vestry Hall, where a gorgeous beadle in plush breeches, white stockings, scarlet cloak trimmed with gold bullion, a wonderful hat, and a wand of office, is standing, and so into the country. Presently we come to the village of Hammersmith, innocent as yet of whelk-stalls and fried-fish shops, and so at last, past Turnham Green, to Brentford.

THE BEADLE.

IX

Brentford was dismissed somewhat summarily in the pages of the BATH ROAD, for which let me here apologise to the county town of Middlesex. Not that I will renounce one jot as to the dirtiness of the place; for what says Gay?—

> Brentford, tedious town,
> For dirty streets and white-legged chickens known.

BRENTFORD.

Now, if Brentford is certainly not tedious nowadays, it is unquestionably as dirty as ever. If you would know the true, poignant, inner meaning of tediousness, you must make acquaintance, say, with Gower Street on a winter's day; a typical street of suburban villas, each 'villa' as like its neighbour as one new sixpence is to another: or the Cromwell Road at any time or under any conditions. Then you will have known tedium. At Brentford, however, all is life, movement, dirt, and balmy odours from a quarter of a mile of roadside gasworks. The bargees and lightermen of this riverside town are swearing picturesquely at one another all day, while the gasmen, the hands at the waterworks, and the railwaymen join in occasionally. Sometimes the profanity so cheerfully bandied about leads to a fight, but not often, because when a bargee addresses his dearest friend by a string of epithets that might make a typical old-time stage-manager blush, it is all taken as a token of friendship. These are the shibboleths of the place.

When, however, Gay alludes to the 'white-legged chickens,' for which, he says, Brentford was known, we are at a loss to identify the breed. That kind of chicken must long since have given up the attempt to be white-legged, and have changed, by process of evolution, into some less easily soiled variety. For the dirt of Brentford is always there. It only varies in kind. In times of drought it makes itself obvious in clouds of black dust, composed of powdered coals and clinkers; and when a day of rain has laid this plague, it is forthwith re-incarnated in the shape of seas of oily black mud. The poet Thomson might have written yesterday—

> E'en so, through Brentford town, a town of mud;

while Dr. Johnson adds his weighty testimony, for when a contemporary, a native of Glasgow, was praising Glasgow to him, the Doctor cut his eloquence with the query: 'Pray, sir, have you ever seen Brentford?' Here was sarcasm indeed! Happily, however, the Glaswegian had *not* seen Brentford, and so was not in a position to appreciate the retort. But Boswell, who, ubiquitous man, was of course present, knew, and told the Doctor this was shocking. 'Why, then, sir,' rejoined Johnson, '*you* have never seen Brentford!'

Then, when we have all this delightful testimony as to Brentford's dirt, comes Shenstone, the melancholy poet who 'found his warmest welcome at an inn,' to testify as to the character of its inhabitants. 'No persons,' says he, 'more solicitous about the preservation of rank than those who have no rank at all. Observe the humours of a country christening; and you will find no court in Christendom so ceremonious as "the quality" of Brentford.'

Despite these criticisms, it must be acknowledged that Brentford is a town of high interest. Its filthy gasworks, its waterworks, its docks have not sufficed to sweep away the old-fashioned appearance of the place. It may, in fact, be safely said that no other such truly picturesque town as Brentford exists near London. This will not long remain true of it, for, even now, new buildings are here and there taking the place of the old. For one thing, Brentford has a quite remarkable number of old inns, and the great stableyards and courtyards of other old coaching hostelries which themselves have disappeared. This was, in fact, the end of the first stage out of London in the coaching era, and the beginning of the last stage in; and in consequence, as befitted a town on the great highway to the West, had ample accommodation, both for man and beast. One of these old yards, indeed,—Red Lion Inn Yard—is historic, for it is traditionally the spot where Edmund Ironside, the king, was murdered by the Danes in 1016, after he had defeated them here. The most famous, however, of all the Brentford inns, the *Three Pigeons*, was brutally demolished many years ago, although it had associations with Shakespeare and 'rare' Ben Jonson. The 'Tumbledown Dick,' another vanished hostelry, whose sign was a satire on the nerveless rule and swift overthrow of the Protector's son, Richard Cromwell, was a well-known house; while the names of some of the old yards—Green Dragon Yard and Catherine Wheel Yard—are reminiscent of once-popular signs.

Then Brentford has the queerest of street names. What think you of 'Half Acre' for the style and title of a thoroughfare? or 'Town Meadow,' which is less a meadow than a slum? Then there are 'The Butts,' with some fine, dignified Queen Anne and Georgian red-brick houses, situated in a quiet spot behind the High Street; and 'The Hollows,' a thoroughfare hollow no longer, if ever it was.

Fronting on to the High Street is the broad and

massive old stone tower of St. Lawrence's Church, the parish church of the so-called 'New' Brentford, itself old beyond compute. The tower dates back four hundred years or so, but the body of the church was rebuilt in Georgian days and is very like, and only a little less hideous than, the gasworks up the street.

An extraordinary story is told by Cyrus Redding, in his *Fifty Years' Recollections*, of a countryman's adventures in London just before the introduction of railways. The adventures began at Brentford: 'I had a relative,' he says, 'who, on stating his intention to come up to town, was solicited to accept as his fellow-traveller a man of property, a neighbour, who had never been thirty miles from home in his life. They travelled by coach. All went well till they reached Brentford, where the countryman supposed he was nearly come to his journey's end. On seeing the lamps mile after mile, he expressed more and more impatience, exclaiming, "Are we not yet in London, and so many miles of lamps?" At length, on reaching Hyde Park Corner, he was told they had arrived. His impatience increased from thence to Lad Lane. He became overwhelmed with astonishment. They entered the "Swan with Two Necks," and my relative bade his companion remain in the coffee-room until he returned. On returning, he found the bird flown, and for six long weeks there were no tidings of him. At length it was discovered that he was in the custody of the constables at Sherborne in Dorsetshire, his mind alienated. He was conveyed home, came partially to his reason for a short time, and died. It was gathered from him that he had become more and more confused at the lights and the long distances he was carried among them; it seemed as if they could have no end. The idea that he could never be extricated from such a labyrinth superseded every other. He could not bear the thought. He went into the street, inquired his way westward, and seemed to have got into Hyde Park, and then out again into the Great Western Road, walking until he could walk no longer. He could relate nothing more that occurred until he was secured. Neither his watch nor money had been taken from him.'

The country-folks who now journey up to town do not behave in this extraordinary fashion on coming to the infinitely greater and more distracting London of to-day.

At the western end of Brentford, just removed from its muddy streets, is Sion, the Duke of Northumberland's suburban residence. The great square embattled stone house stands in the midst of the park, screened from observation from the road by great clusters of forest trees. Through the ornamental classic stone screen and iron gateway, erected in the well-known 'Adam style' by John Adam about 1780, the green sward may be glimpsed; the fresher and more beautiful by contrast with the dusty high-road. Above the arched stone entrance stands the Percy Lion, *statant*, as heralds would say, with tail extended.

Sion is well named, for no fairer scene can be imagined than this in the long days of summer, when the lovely gardens are at their best and the Thames flows by the park with glittering golden ripples. The Daughters of Sion, whose religious retreat this was, belonged to the Order of St. Bridget. Their abbey, with its lands and great revenues, was suppressed and confiscated by Henry the Eighth in 1532. Nine years later his Queen, Katherine Howard, was imprisoned within the desecrated walls before being handed over to the headsman, and in another seven years the body of the King himself lay here a night on its journey to Windsor. There is a horrid story that tells how the unwieldy corpse of the bloated royal monster burst, and how the dogs drank his blood.

In the reign of his daughter, Queen Mary, Sion enjoyed a few years' restitution of its rights and property, but when Elizabeth ascended the throne, the 'Daughters' were finally dispossessed. They wandered to Flanders, and thence, by devious ways, and with many hardships, eventually to Lisbon. The Abbey of Sion yet exists there, and the sisters are still solely Englishwomen. It is on record that they still cherish the hope of returning to their lost home by the banks of the Thames, and have to this day the keys of that abbey. Seventy years or so since, the then Duke of Northumberland, travelling in Portugal, called upon them, and was told of this fond belief. They even showed him the keys. But he was equal to the occasion, and cynically remarked that the locks had been altered since those days!

X

Hounslow, to which we now come, being situated, like all the other places between this and Hyde Park Corner, on the Bath Road, as well as on the road

THE 'BELL,' HOUNSLOW.

to Exeter, has been referred to at some length in the book on that highway. Coming to the place again, there seems no reason to alter or add much to what was said in those pages. The long, long uninteresting street is just as sordid as ever, and the very few houses of any note facing it are fewer. There remains, it is true, that old coaching inn, the 'George,' modernised with discretion, and at the parting of the ways the gallows-like sign of the 'Bell' still keeps its place on the footpath, with the old original bell still depending from it, although, at the moment of writing, the house itself is being pulled down. But the angle where the roads divide is under revision, and the hoardings that now hide from sight the old shops and the red-brick house, with high-pitched roof and dormer windows, that has stood here so long, will give place shortly to some modern building with plate-glass shop-fronts and a general air of aggressive modernity which will be another link gone with the Hounslow of the past. Thus it is that an illustration is shown here of the 'parting of the ways' before the transformation is complete; for although the fork of the roads leading to places so distant from this point, and from one another, as Bath and Exeter must needs always lend something to the imagination, yet a commonplace modern street building cannot, for another hundred years, command respect or be worth sketching, even for the sake of the significant spot on which it stands.

The would-be decorative gas-lamp that stands here in the centre of the road bears two tin tablets inscribed respectively, 'To Slough' and 'To Staines,' in a somewhat parochial fashion. They had no souls, those people who inscribed these legends. Did they not know that we stand here upon highways famed in song and story; not merely the flat and uninteresting seven and ten miles respectively to Staines and Slough, but the hundred and fifty-five miles to Exeter and the ninety-five miles to Bath!

Here, then, we see the Bath Road going off to the

HOUNSLOW: THE PARTING OF THE WAYS.

right and the Exeter Road to the left in semi-suburban fashion. Had it not been for the winter fogs this level stretch would have invariably been the delight of the old coachmen; but when the roads were wrapped in obscurity they were hard put to it to keep on the highway. Sometimes they did not even succeed in doing so, but drove instead into the noisome ditches, filled with evil-smelling black mud, which at that time divided the road from Hounslow Heath.

Charles Ward, whom the coaching critics of his age united to honour as an artist with 'the ribbons,' drove the famous Exeter 'Telegraph' the thirty miles to Bagshot, reaching that village usually at 11 P.M., and taking the up coach from thence to London at four o'clock in the morning. He tells how in the winter the mails had often to be escorted out of London with flaring torches, seven or eight mails following one another, the guard of the foremost lighting the one following, and so on, travelling at a slow pace, like a funeral procession. 'Many times,' he says, 'I have been three hours going from London to Hounslow. I remember one very foggy night, instead of arriving at Bagshot at eleven o'clock, I did not get there till one in the morning. On my way back to town, when the fog was very bad, I was coming over Hounslow Heath, when I reached the spot where the old powder-mills used to stand. I saw several lights in the road and heard voices which induced me to stop. The old Exeter mail, which left Bagshot thirty minutes before I did, had met with a singular accident. It was driven by a man named Gambier: his leaders had come in contact with a hay-cart on its way to London, which caused them to suddenly turn round, break the pole, and blunder down a steep embankment, at the bottom of which was a narrow deep ditch, filled with water and mud. The mail coach pitched on the stump of a willow tree that overhung the ditch; the coachman and the outside passengers were thrown over into the meadow beyond, and the horses went into the ditch. The unfortunate wheelers were drowned or smothered in the mud. There were two inside passengers, who were extricated with some difficulty, but fortunately no one was injured. I managed to take the passengers with the guard and mail bags on to London, leaving the coachman to wait for daylight before he could make an attempt to get the mail up the embankment. They endeavoured to accomplish this with cart horses and chains, and they had nearly reached the top of the bank when something gave way, and the poor old mail went back into the ditch again. I shall never forget the scene. There were about a dozen men from the powder-mills trying to render assistance, and with their black faces, each bearing a torch in his hand, they presented a curious spectacle. This happened about 1840. Posts and rails were erected at the spot after the accident. I passed the place in 1870, and they were there still, as well as the old pollard willow stump.'

The old-time associations of Hounslow Heath are almost forgotten now, for, where Claude du Vall and Dick Turpin waited patiently for travellers, there are nowadays long rows of suburban villas which have long since changed the dreary scene. Nothing so romantic as the meeting of the lawyer with the redoubtable Dick is likely to befall the traveller in these times :—

As Turpin was riding on Hounslow Heath,
A lawyer there he chanced for to meet,
Who said, 'Kind sir, ain't you afraid
Of Turpin, that mischievous blade?'

'Oh! no, sir,' says Turpin, 'I've been more acute,
I've hidden my money all in my boot.'
'And mine,' says the lawyer, 'the villain can't find,
For I have sewed it into my cape behind.'

They rode till they came to the Powder Mill,
When Turpin bid the lawyer for to stand still.
'Good sir,' quoth he, 'that cape must come off,
For my horse stands in need of a saddle-cloth.'

'Ah, well,' says the lawyer, 'I'm very compliant,
I'll put it all right with my next coming client.'
'Then,' says Turpin, 'we're both of a trade, never doubt it,
Only you rob by law, and I rob without it.'

The last vestige is gone of the bleak and barren aspect of the road, and even the singular memorial of a murder, which, according to the writer of a road-book published in 1802, stood near by, has vanished: 'Upon a spot of Hounslow Heath, about a stone's throw from the road, on leaving that village, a small wood monument is shockingly marked with a bloody hand and knife, and the following inscription: "Buried with a stake through his body here, the wicked murderer, John Pretor, who cut the throat of his wife and child, and poisoned himself, July 6, 1765."'

It is a splendidly surfaced road that runs hence to Staines, and the fact is sufficiently well known for it to be crowded on Saturday afternoons and Sundays with cyclists of the 'scorcher' variety, members of cycling clubs out for a holiday, and taking their

THE 'GREEN MAN,' HATTON.

pleasure at sixteen miles an hour, Indian file, hanging on to one another's back wheel, with shoulders humped over handle-bars and eyes for nothing but the road surface.

But there are quiet, deserted bye-lanes where these highway crowds never come. Just such a lane is that which leads off here, by the river Crane and the Bedfont Powder Mills, to the right, and makes for Hatton—'Hatton-in-the-Hinterland,' one might well call it.

Have you ever been to Hatton? Have you, indeed, ever even heard of it? I suppose not, for Hatton is a remote hamlet, tucked away in that triangular corner of Middlesex situated between the branching Bath and Exeter Roads which is practically unexplored. Yet the place, after the uninteresting, unrelieved flatness of the market gardens that stretch for miles around, is almost pretty. It boasts a few isolated houses, and has (what is more to the point in this connection) a neat and cheerful-looking old inn, fronted by a large horse-pond.

The 'Green Man' at Hatton looks nowadays a guileless place, with no secrets, and yet it possesses behind that innocent exterior a veritable highwayman's hiding-place. This retiring-place of modest worth, eager to escape from the embarrassing attentions of the outer world, may be seen by the curious traveller in the little bar-parlour on the left hand as you enter the front door.

It is a narrow, low-ceiled room, with an old-fashioned fire-grate in it, filling what was once a huge chimney-corner. At the back of this grate is a hole leading to a passage which gives access to a cavernous nook in the thickness of the wall. Through this hole, decently covered at most times with an innocent-looking fire-back, crawled those exquisite knights of the road, what time the Bow Street runners were questing almost at their heels.

And here, it is related, one of these fine fellows nearly revealed his presence while the officers of the law were refreshing themselves with a dram in that room. What with a cold in the head, and the accumulated soot and dust of his hiding-place, he could not help sneezing, although his very life

THE HIGHWAYMAN'S RETREAT, THE 'GREEN MAN.'

depended on the question 'To sneeze or not to sneeze.'

The minions of the law were not so far gone in liquor but that they heard the muffled sound of that sneeze, and it took all the landlord's eloquence to persuade them that it was the cat!

Where footpads and highwaymen lurked on the

scrubby heath, and the troopers of King James the Second, sent here to overawe London, lay encamped, there stretch nowadays the broad market gardens, where in spring-time the yellow daffodils, and in early summer the wallflowers, are grown by the acre for Covent Garden and the delight of Londoners. Orchards and vast fields of vegetables take up almost all the rest of the reclaimed waste, and if the country for many miles be indeed as flat as, or flatter than, your hand, and with never a tree but the scraggy hedgerow elms that grow here in such fantastic shapes, why amends are made in the scent of the blossoms, the bounteous promise of nature, and in the free and open air that resounds with the gladsome shrilling of the lark.

These market gardens that surround London have an interest all their own. Such scenes as that of Millet's 'Angelus'—the rough toil, that is to say, without the devotion—are the commonplaces of these wide fields, stretching away, level, to the horizon. All day long the men, women, and children are working, according to the season, in the damp, heavy clay, or in the sun-baked rows of growing produce, digging, hoeing, sowing, weeding, or gathering the cabbages, potatoes, peas, lettuces, and beans that go to furnish the myriad tables of the 'Wen of wens,' as Cobbett savagely calls London. He thought very little of Hounslow Heath, which he describes as 'a sample of all that is bad in soil and villainous in look. Yet,' he says, writing in 1825, 'all this is now enclosed, and what they call "cultivated."'

What they *call* cultivated! That is indeed

excellent. It would be well if Cobbett could take a 'Rural Ride' over the Heath to-day and see this cultivation, not merely so called, which raises some of the finest market-garden produce ever seen, and supplies London with the most beautiful spring blossoms. If it would not suffice to see the growing crops, it would perhaps be better to watch the loading of the clumsy market waggons with the gathered wealth of the soil. Tier upon tier of cabbages, neatly packed to an alarming height; bundles of the finest lettuces; bushels of peas; in short, a bounteous quantity of every domestic vegetable you care to name, being packed for the lumbering, rumbling, three-miles-an-hour journey overnight from the market gardens to the early morning babel of Covent Garden.

The market waggons, going to London, or returning about eight o'clock in the morning, form, in short, one of the most characteristic features of the first fifteen miles of this road. The waggoners, more often than not asleep, are jogged up to town by the philosophic horses who know the way just as well as the blinking fellows who are supposed to drive them. Drive them? One can just imagine the horse-laughs of those particularly knowing animals, who move along quite independently of the reclining figure above, stretched full length, face downwards, on the mountainous pile of smelly cabbages, if the idea could be conveyed to them.

There is an exquisite touch of appropriateness in the fact that on converted Hounslow Heath, where these terrors of the peaceful traveller formerly practised their unlicensed trade, reformatories should be nowadays established. One of them, called by the prettier name of the 'Feltham Industrial School,' is placed just to the south of the road, near East Bedfont. It houses and educates for honest careers the young criminals and the waifs and strays brought before the Middlesex magistrates. The neighbourhood of this huge institution is made evident to the traveller across these widespreading levels by the strange sight of a full-sized, fully-rigged ship on the horizon. The stranger who journeys this way and has always supposed Hounslow Heath to be anything rather than the neighbour to a seaport, feels in some doubt as to the evidence of his senses or the accuracy of his geographical recollections. Strange, he thinks, that he should have forgotten the sea estuary on which the Heath borders, or the ship canal that traverses these wilds. But if he inquires of any one with local knowledge whom he may meet, he will learn that this is the model training-ship built in the grounds of the Industrial School. The 'Endeavour,' as she is called, if not registered A1 at Lloyd's, or not at all a seaworthy craft, is at any rate well found in the technical details of masts and spars, and the rigging appropriate to a schooner-rigged Blackwall liner. Those among the seven hundred or so of the young vagabonds who are being educated here in the way they should go—those among them who think they would like a life on the bounding main, are here taught to climb the rigging with the agility of cats; to furl the sails or shake them free, or to keep a sharp look-out for the iron reefs that lurk on the inhospitable coasts of Hounslow Heath, lest all on board should be cast away and utterly undone. It is an odd experience to walk around the great hull, half submerged — half buried, that is to say—in the asphalt paths of the parade ground, but the oddest experiences must be those of the boys who, when they get aboard a floating ship, come to it thoroughly trained in everything save 'sea-legs' and the keeping of an easy stomach when the breezes blow and the surges rock the vessel.

XII

The village of East Bedfont, three miles from Hounslow, is a picturesque surprise, after the long flat road. The highway suddenly broadens out here, and gives place to a wide village green, with a pond, and real ducks! and an even more real village church whose wooden extinguisher spire peeps out from a surrounding cluster of trees, and from behind a couple of fantastically clipped yews guarding the churchyard gate.

The 'Bedfont Peacocks,' as they are called, are not so perfect as they were when first cut in 1704, for the trimming of them was long neglected, and these curiously clipped evergreens require constant attention. The date on one side, and the churchwardens' initials of the period on the other, once standing out boldly, are now only to be discerned by the Eye of Faith. The story of the Peacocks is that they were cut at the costs and charges of a former inhabitant of the village, who, proposing in turn to two sisters also living here, was scornfully refused by them. They were, says the legend, 'as proud as peacocks,' and the mortified suitor chose this spiteful method of typifying the fact. Of course, the story was retailed to travellers on passing through Bedfont by every

EAST BEDFONT

coachman and guard; nor, indeed, would it be at all surprising to learn that they, in fact, really invented it, for they were masters in the art of romancing. So the fame of the Peacocks grew. An old writer at once celebrates them, and the then landlord of the 'Black Dog,' in the rather neat verse:

> Harvey, whose inn commands a view
> Of Bedfont's church and churchyard too,
> Where yew-trees into peacocks shorn,
> In vegetable torture mourn.

At length they were immortalised by Hood, the elder, in a quite serious poem :—

Where erst two haughty maidens used to be,
  In pride of plume, where plumy Death hath trod,
Trailing their gorgeous velvet wantonly,
  Most unmeet pall, over the holy sod ;
There, gentle stranger, thou may'st only see
  Two sombre peacocks. Age, with sapient nod,
Marking the spot, still tarries to declare
  How once they lived, and wherefore they are there.

Alas ! that breathing vanity should go
  Where pride is buried ; like its very ghost,
Unrisen from the naked bones below,
  In novel flesh, clad in the silent boast
Of gaudy silk that flutters to and fro,
  Shedding its chilling superstition most
On young and ignorant natures as is wont
  To haunt the peaceful churchyard of Bedfont !

If any one can unravel the sense from the tangled lines of the second verse,—as obscure as some of Browning's poetry—let him account himself clever.

The 'Black Dog,' once the halting-place of the long extinct 'Driving Club,' of which the late Duke of Beaufort was a member, has recently been demolished. A large villa stands on the site of it, at the corner of the Green, as the village is left behind.

The flattest of flat, and among the straightest of straight roads is this which runs from East Bedfont into Staines. That loyal bard, John Taylor, the 'Water Poet,' was along this route on his way to the Isle of Wight in 1647. He started from the 'Rose,' in Holborn, on Thursday, 19th October, in the Southampton coach :—

We took one coach, two coachmen, and four horses,
And merrily from London made our courses,
We wheel'd the top of the heavy hill call'd Holborn
(Up which hath been full many a sinful soul borne),
And so along we jolted to St. Giles's,
Which place from Brentford six, or nearly seven, miles is,
To Staines that night at five o'clock we coasted,
Where, at the Bush, we had bak'd, boil'd, and roasted.

XIII

Staines, where the road leaves Middlesex and crosses the Thames into Surrey, is almost as commonplace a little town as it is possible to find within the home counties. Late Georgian and Early Victorian stuccoed villas and square, box-like, quite uninteresting houses struggle for numerical superiority over later buildings in the long High Street, and the contest is not an exciting one. Staines, sixteen miles from London, is, in fact, of that nondescript 'neither fish, flesh, fowl, nor good red-herring'—character that belongs to places situated in the marches of town and country. Almost everything of interest has vanished, and although the railway has come to Staines, it has not brought with it the life and bustle that are generally conferred by railways on places near London. But, of course, Staines is on the London and South-Western Railway, which explains everything.

Staines disputes with Colnbrook, on the Bath Road, the honour of having been the Roman station of *Ad Pontes*, and has the best of it, according to the views of the foremost authorities. 'At the Bridges' would doubtless have been an excellently descriptive name for either place, in view of the number of streams at both, and the bridges necessary to cross them; but the very name of Staines should of itself be almost sufficient to prove the Roman origin of the place, even if the Roman remains found in and about it were not considered conclusive evidence. There are those who derive 'Staines' from the ancient stone still standing on the north bank of the Thames, above the bridge, marking the historic boundary up-stream of the jurisdiction exercised over the river by the City of London; but there can be no doubt of its real origin in the paved Roman highway, a branch of the Akeman Street, on which this former military station of *Ad Pontes* stood. The stones of the old road yet remained when the Saxons overran the country, and it was named 'the Stones' by that people, from the fact of being on a paved highway. The very many places in this county with the prefixes, Stain, Stone, Stan, Street, Streat, and Stret, all, or nearly all, originate in the paved Roman roads (or 'streets') and fords; and there is little to support another theory, that the name of Staines came from a Roman *milliarium*, or milestone, which may or may not have stood somewhere here on the road.

The stone column, very like a Roman altar, standing on three steps and a square panelled plinth, and placed in a meadow on the north bank of the river, is known variously as 'Staines Stone,' and 'London Stone.' It marks the place where the upper and lower Thames meet; is the boundary line of Middlesex and Buckinghamshire; and is also the boundary mark of the Metropolitan Police District. Besides these manifold and important offices, it also delimits the western boundary of the area comprised within the old London Coal and Wine Duties Acts, by which a tax, similar to the *octroi* still in force at the outskirts of many Continental towns, was levied on all coals, coke, and cinders, and all wines, entering London. Renewed from time to time, the imposts were finally abolished in 1889, but the old posts with cast-iron inscriptions detailing the number and date of the several Acts of Parliament under which these dues were levied, are still to be found beside the roads, rivers, and canals around London.

Much weather-worn and dilapidated, 'London Stone' still retains long inscriptions giving the names of the Lord Mayors who have officially visited the spot as *ex-officio* chairmen of the Thames Conservancy:—

> Conservators of Thames from mead to mead,
> Great guardians of small sprites that swim the flood,
> Warders of London Stone,

as Tom Hood mock-heroically sings.

Above all is the deeply cut aspiration, 'God Preserve the City of London, A.D. 1280.' The pious prayer has been answered, and six hundred and twenty years later the City has been, like David, delivered out of the hands of the spoiler and from the enemies that compassed it round about; by which Royal Commissions and the London County Council may be understood.

If the Roman legionaries could return to *Ad*

THE STAINES STONE.

Pontes and see Staines Bridge and the hideous iron girder bridge by which the London and South-Western Railway crosses the Thames they would be genuinely astonished. The first-named, which is the stone bridge built by Rennie in 1832, carries the

Exeter Road over the river, and is of a severe classic aspect which might find favour with the resurrected Romans; but what *could* they think of the other?

We may see an additional importance in this situation of *Ad Pontes* in the fact that between Staines Bridge and London Bridge there was anciently no other passage across the river, save by the hazardous expedient of fording it at certain points. The only way to the West of England in mediaeval times, it was then of wood, and zealously kept in repair by the grant of trees from the Royal Forest of Windsor and by the *pontage*, or bridge toll levied from passengers. Still, it was often broken down by floods. The poet Gay, in his *Journey to Exeter*, says, passing Hounslow:—

> Thence, o'er wide shrubby heaths, and furrowed lanes,
> We come, where Thames divides the meads of Staines.
> We ferried o'er; for late the Winter's flood
> Shook her frail bridge, and tore her piles of wood.

That would probably have been about the year 1720. In 1791 an Act of Parliament authorised the building of a new bridge, and accordingly a stone structure was begun, and eventually opened in 1797. This had to be demolished, almost immediately, owing to a failure of one of its piers, and an iron bridge was built in its stead, presently to meet with much the same fate. This, then, gave place to the existing bridge.

The 'Vine Inn,' which once stood by the bridge and was a welcome sight to travellers, has disappeared, together with most of the old hostelries that once rendered Staines a town of inns. Gone, too, is the 'Bush,' and others, although not demolished, have either retired into private life, or are disguised as commonplace shops. The 'Angel' still remains, but not the 'Blue Boar,' kept, according to Dean Swift, by the quarrelsome couple, Phyllis and John. Phyllis had run away from home on her wedding morn with John, who was her father's groom, and a good-for-naught. At the inn they were installed at last, John as the drunken landlord, Phyllis as the kind landlady :—

> They keep at Staines the Old Blue Boar,
> Are cat and dog—

and other things unfitted for ears polite.

The church is without interest, but there lies in its churchyard, among the other saints and sinners, Lady Letitia Lade, the foul-mouthed cast-off *chère amie* of the Prince Regent, who married her off to John Lade, his coachman, whom he knighted for his complaisance.

XIV

Staines is no sooner left behind than we come to Egham, once devoted almost wholly to the coaching interest, then the scene of suburban race-meetings, and now that those blackguardly orgies have been suppressed, just a dead-alive suburb — dusty, uninteresting. The old church has been modernised, and the old coaching inns either mere beer-shops or else improved away altogether. The last one to remain in its old form—the 'Catherine Wheel'—has recently lost all its old roadside character, and has become very much up-to-date.

Here we are upon the borders of Windsor Great Park, and a road turning off to the right hand leads beside the Thames to Old Windsor, past Cooper's Hill and within sight of Runemede and Magna Charta island, where the 'Palladium of our English liberties' was wrung from the unwilling King John. A public reference to the 'Palladium' used unfailingly to 'bring down the house,' but it has been left to the present generation to view the very spot where it was granted, not only without a quickening of the pulse, but with the suspicion of a yawn. You cannot expect reverence from people who possibly saw King John as the central and farcical figure of last year's pantomime, with a low-comedy nose and an expression of ludicrous terror, handing Magna Charta to baronial supers armoured with polished metal dish-covers for breastplates and saucepans for helmets. 'Nothing is sacred to a sapper,' is a saying that arose in Napoleon's campaigns. Let us, in these piping times of peace, change the figure, and say, 'Nothing is sacred to a librettist.'

Long years before Egham ever became a coaching village, in the dark ages of road travel, when inns were scarce and travellers few, the 'Bells of Ouseley,' the old-fashioned riverside inn along this bye-road, was a place of greater note than it is now. Although forgotten by the crowds who keep the high-road, it is an inn happier in its situation than most, for it stands on the banks of the Thames at one of its most picturesque points, just below Old Windsor.

The sign, showing five bells on a blue ground, derives its name from the once-famed bells of the long-demolished Oseney Abbey at Oxford, celebrated,

THE 'BELLS OF OUSELEY.'

before the Reformation swept them away, for their silvery tones, which are said to have surpassed even those

> Bells of Shandon
> Which sound so grand on
> The pleasant waters of the River Lea,

of which 'Father Prout' sang some forty-five years ago. The abbey, however, possessed *six* bells. They were named Douce, Clement, Austin, Hauctetor, Gabriel, and John.

The 'Bells of Ouseley' had at one time a reputation for a very much less innocent thing than picturesqueness, for a hundred and fifty years ago, or thereabouts, it was very popular with the worst class of footpads, who were used to waylay travellers by the shore, or on the old Bath and Exeter Roads, and, robbing them, were not content, but, practically applying the axiom that 'dead men tell no tales,' gave their victims a knock over the head, and, tying them in sacks, heaved them into the river. These be legends, and legends are not always truthful, but it is a fact that, some years ago, when the Thames Conservancy authorities were dredging the bed of the river just here, they found the remains of a sack and the perfect skeleton of a human being.

XV

Regarding the country through which the road passes, between Kensington, Egham, Sunningdale, Virginia Water, and Bagshot, Cobbett has some characteristic things to say. Between Hammersmith and Egham it is 'as flat as a pancake,' and the soil 'a nasty stony dirt upon a bed of gravel.' Sunninghill and Sunningdale, 'all made into "grounds" and gardens by tax-eaters,' are at the end of a 'blackguard heath,' and are 'not far distant from the Stock-jobbing crew. The roads are level, and they are smooth. The wretches can go from the "'Change" without any danger to their worthless necks.'

There are now, sad to say, after the lapse of nearly eighty years, a great many more of the 'crew' here, and they journey to and from Capel Court with even less danger to their necks, bad luck to them!

Egham Hill surmounted, the Holloway College for Women is a prominent object on the left-hand side of the road, the fad of Thomas Holloway, whose thumping big fortune was derived from the advertising enterprise which lasted wellnigh two generations, and during the most of that period rendered the advertisement columns of London and provincial papers hideous with beastly illustrations of suppurating limbs, and the horrid big type inquiry, 'Have you a Bad Leg?' Pills and ointments, what sovereign specifics you are—towards the accumulation of wealth! All-powerful unguents, how beneficent—towards the higher education of woman!

No less a sum than £600,000 was expended on the building and equipment of this enormous range of buildings, opened in 1887, and provided royally with everything a college requires except students, whose number yet falls far short of the three hundred and fifty the place is calculated to house and teach. A fine collection of the works of modern English painters is to be seen here, where study is made easy for the 'girl graduates' by the provision of luxuriously appointed class-rooms and shady nooks where 'every pretty domina can study the phenomena' of integral calculus and other domestic sciences. It seems a waste of good money that, although a sum equal to £500 a year for each student is expended on the higher education of women here, no prophetess has yet issued from Egham with a message for the world; and that, consequently, Mr. Thomas Holloway and his medicated grease have as yet missed that posthumous fame for which so big a bid was made.

In two miles Virginia Water is reached, passing on the right hand the plantations of Windsor Great Park. To this spot runs every day in summer-time the 'Old Times' coach, which, first put on this road in the spring of 1879, kept running every season until 1886, when it was transferred to the Brighton Road, there to become famous through Selby's historic 'record' drive. Another coach, called the 'Express,' was put on the Virginia Water trip in 1886 and 1887; but, following upon Selby's death in the November of the latter year, the 'Old Times' was reinstated on this route, and has been running ever since, leaving the Hotel Victoria, Northumberland Avenue, every week-day morning for the 'Wheatsheaf,' and returning in the evening.

This same 'Wheatsheaf' is probably one of the very ugliest houses that ever bedevilled a country road, and looks like a great public-house wrenched bodily from London streets and dropped down here at a venture. But it is for all that a very popular place with the holiday-makers who come here to explore the beauties and the curiosities of Virginia Water.

There are artificial lakes here, just within the Park of Windsor—lakes which give the place its name, and made so long ago that Nature in her kindly way has obliterated all traces of their artificiality. It is a hundred years since this pleasance of Virginia Water was formed by imprisoning the rivulets that run into this hollow, and banking up the end of it; nearly a hundred years since the Ruined Temple was built as a ready-made ruin; and there is no more, nor indeed any other such, delightful spot near London. It is quite a pity to come by the knowledge that the ruins were imported from Greece and Carthage, because without that knowledge who knows what romance could not be weaved around those graceful columns, amid the waters and the wilderness? Beyond Virginia Water we come to Sunningdale.

From Turnham Green to Staines, and thence to Shrub's Hill we are on the old Roman Road to that famous town which has been known at different periods of its existence as Aquae Solis, Akemanceaster, and Bath. The Saxons called the road Akeman Street. Commencing at a junction with the Roman Watling Street at the point where the Marble Arch now stands, it proceeded along the Bayswater Road, and so by Notting Hill, past Shepherd's Bush, and along the Goldhawk Road, where, instead of turning sharply to the left like the existing road that leads to Young's Corner, it continued its straight course through the district now occupied by the modern artistic colony of Bedford Park, falling into the present Chiswick High Road somewhere between Turnham Green and Gunnersbury. Through Brentford, Hounslow, and Staines the last vestiges of the actual Roman Road were lost in the alterations carried out for the improvement of the highway under the provisions of the Hounslow and Basingstoke Road Improvement Act of 1728, but there can be little doubt that the road traffic of to-day from Hounslow to Shrub's Hill follows in the tracks of the pioneers who built the original road in A.D. 43; while as for old-world Brentford, it would surprise no one if the veritable Roman paving were found deep down below its High Street, long buried in the silt and mud that have raised the level of the highway at the ford from which the place-name derives.

The present West of England road turns off from the Akeman Street at the bend in the highway at Shrub's Hill, leaving the Roman way to continue in an unfaltering straight line across the scrubby wastes and solitudes of Broadmoor, to Finchampstead, Stratfieldsaye, and Silchester. It is there known to the country folk as the 'Nine Mile Ride' and the 'Devil's Highway.' The prefix of the place-name 'Stratfieldsaye,' as a matter of fact, derives from its situation on this 'street.' Silchester is the site of the Roman city *Calleva Atrebatum*, and the excavated ruins of this British Pompeii prove how important a place this was, standing as it did at the fork of the roads leading respectively to *Aquae Solis*, and to *Isca Damnoniorum*, the Exeter of a later age. Branching off here to *Isca*, the Roman road was for the rest of the way to the West known as the *Via Iceniana*, the Icen Way, and was perhaps regarded as a continuation of what is now called the Icknield Street, the road which runs diagonally to Norfolk and Suffolk, the country of the Iceni.

Very little of this old Roman road on its way to the West is identical with any of the three existing routes to Exeter. There is that length just named, from Gunnersbury to Shrub's Hill; another piece, a mile or so from Andover onward, by the Weyhill route; the crossing of the modern highway between 'Woodyates Inn' and Thorney Down; and from Dorchester to Bridport, where, as Gay says of his cavaliers' journey to Exeter:—

> Now on true Roman way our horses sound,
> Graevius would kneel and kiss the sacred ground.

Onwards to Exeter the measurements of Antoninus and his fellows—those literally 'classic' forerunners of Ogilby, Cary, Paterson, and Mogg—are hazy in the extreme, and it is difficult to say how the Roman road entered into the Queen City of the West.

Oh! for one hour with the author of the Antonine Itinerary, to settle the vexed questions of routes and stations along this road to the country of the Dumnonii. 'Here,' one would say to him, 'is your starting-point, *Londinium*, which we call London. Very good; now kindly tell us whether we are correct in giving Staines as the place you call *Ad Pontes*; and is Egham the site of *Bibracte?* *Calleva* we have identified with Silchester, but where was your next station, *Vindomis?* Was it St. Mary Bourne?'

In the meanwhile, until spiritualism becomes more of an exact science, we must be content with our own deductions, and, with the aid of the Ordnance map, trace the Roman *Via Iceniana* by Quarley Hill and Grateley to the hill of Old Sarum, which is readily identified as the station of *Sorbiodunum*. Thence it goes by Stratford Toney to 'Woodyates Inn' and Gussage Cow Down, where the utterly vanished *Vindogladia* is supposed to have stood. Between this and Dorchester there was another post whose name and position are alike unknown, although the course of the road may yet be faintly traced past the fortified hill of Badbury Rings, the *Mons Badonicus* of King Arthur's defeat, to Tincleton and Stinsford, and so into Dorchester, the *Durnovaria* of the Romans, through what was the Eastgate of that city. The names and sites of two more stations westward are lost, and the situation of *Moridunum*, the next-named post, is so uncertain that such widely sundered places as Seaton, on the Dorset coast, and Honiton, in Devon, eighteen miles farther, are given for it. Morecomblake, a mile from Seaton, is, however, the most likely site. Thence, on to Exeter, this Roman military way is lost.

XVI

From Virginia Water up to the crest of Shrub's Hill, Sunningdale, is a distance of a mile and a quarter, and beyond, all the way into Bagshot, is a region of sand and fir-trees and attempts at cultivation, varied by newly-built villas, where considerable colonies of Cobbett's detested stock-jobbers and other business men from the 'Wen of wens' have set up country quarters. And away to right and left, for miles upon miles, stretches that wild country known variously as Bagshot and Ascot Heaths and Chobham Ridges.

The extensive and dreary-looking tract of land,

still wild and barren for the most part, called Bagshot Heath, has during the last century been the scene of many attempts made to bring it under cultivation. These populous times are ill-disposed to the continued existence of waste and unproductive lands, which, when near London, are especially valuable, if they can be made to grow anything at all. One thing which, above all others, has led to the beginning of the end of these old-time wildernesses, formerly the haunts of highwaymen, is the modern discovery of the country and of the benefits of fresh air. When the nineteenth century was yet young the townsman still retained the old habits of thought which regarded the heaths and the hills with aversion. He pigged away his existence over his shop or warehouse in the City, and thought the country fit only for the semi-savages who grew the fruit and vegetables that helped to supply his table, or cultivated the wheat of which his daily bread was compounded. It has been left to us, his descendants, to love the wilds, and thus it is that villa homes are springing up amid the heaths and the pines of this region, away from Woking on the south to Ascot in the north.

One comes downhill into the large village or small (very small) town of Bagshot, which gives a name to these surrounding wastes of scrubby grass, gorse, and fir-trees. The now quiet street faces the road in the hollow, across which runs the Bourne brook that perhaps originated the place-name, 'Beck-shot' being the downhill rush of the stream or beck. The many 'shotts' that terminate the names of places in Hants and Surrey have this common origin, and are similarly situated in the little hollows watered by descending brooks.

Bagshot has nearly forgotten the old coaching days in the growing importance of its military surroundings, and most of its once celebrated inns have retired into private life, all except the 'King's Arms.'

The ground to the north of the Exeter Road, on

BAGSHOT.

the west of Bagshot village, was once a peat moor. Hazel-nuts and bog-oak were often dug up there. Then began the usual illegal encroachments on what was really common land, and stealthily the moor was enclosed and subsequently converted into a nursery-ground for rhododendrons, which flourish amazingly on this soil when it has once been trenched. Beneath the black sand which usually covers this ground there frequently occurs a very hard iron rust, or thin stratum of oxide of iron, which prevents drainage of the soil, with a blue sandy clay underlying. This stratum of iron rust requires to be broken through, and the blue clay subsoil raised to the surface and mixed with the black sand, before anything will grow here.

There is to be seen on the summit of the steep hill that leads out of Bagshot an old inn called the 'Jolly Farmer.' This is the successor of a still older house which stood at the side of the road, and was famous in the annals of highway robbery, having been once the residence of William Davis, the notorious 'Golden Farmer,' who lived here in the century before last.

The agriculturist with this auriferous name was a man greatly respected in the neighbourhood, and acquired the nickname from his invariable practice of paying his bills in gold. He was never known to tender cheques, bank-notes, or bills, and this fact was considered so extraordinary that it excited much comment, while at the same time increasing the respect due to so substantial a man. But respect at last fell from Mr. William Davis like a cloak; for one night when a coach was robbed (as every coach was robbed then) on Bagshot Heath by a peculiar highwayman who had earned a great reputation from his invariable practice of returning all the jewellery and notes and keeping only the coin, the masked robber, departing with his plunder, was shot in the back by a traveller who had managed to secrete a pistol.

Bound hand and foot, the wounded highwayman was hauled into the lighted space before the entrance to the 'King's Arms,' when the gossips of the place recognised in him the well-known features of the

'Golden Farmer.' A ferocious Government, which had no sympathy with highway robbery, caused the 'Golden Farmer' to be hanged and afterwards gibbeted at his own threshold.

The present inn, an ugly building facing down the road, does not occupy the site of the old house, which stood on the right hand, going westwards. A table, much hacked and mutilated, standing in the parlour of the 'Jolly Farmer,' came from the highwayman's vanished home. A tall obelisk that stood on the triangular green at the fork of the roads here—where the signpost is standing nowadays—has long since disappeared. It was a prominent landmark in the old coaching days, and was inscribed with the distances of many towns from this spot. A still existing link with the times of the highwaymen is the so-called 'Claude du Vall's Cottage,' which stands in the heathy solitudes at some distance along Lightwater Lane, to the right-hand of the road. The cottage, of which there is no doubt that it often formed a hiding-place for that worthy, has lost its ancient thatch, and is now covered with commonplace slates.

Almost immediately after leaving the 'Jolly Farmer' behind, the road grows hateful, passing in succession the modern townships of Cambridge Town Camberley, and York Town. The exact point where one of these modern squatting-places of those who hang on to the skirts of Tommy Atkins joins another may be left to local experts; to the traveller they present the appearance of one long and profoundly depressing street.

Cobbett knew the road well, and liked this shabby

line of military settlements little. Coming up to 'the Wen' in 1821, and passing Blackwater, he reached York Town, and thus he holds forth: '*After pleasure comes pain*,' says Solomon, and after the sight of Lady Mildmay's truly noble plantations (at Hartley Row) came that of the clouts of the 'gentleman cadets' of the '*Royal Military College of Sandhurst!*' Here, close by the roadside, is the *drying ground*. Sheets, shirts, and all sorts of things were here spread upon lines covering perhaps an acre of ground! We soon afterwards came to '*York* Place' on '*Osnaburg* Hill.' And is there never to be an *end* of these things? Away to the left we see that immense building which contains children *breeding up to be military commanders!* Has this place cost so little as two millions of pounds? I never see this place (and I have seen it forty times during the last twenty years) without asking myself this question, 'Will this thing be suffered to go on; will this thing, created by money *raised by loan;* will this thing be upheld by means of taxes *while the interest of the Debt is reduced*, on the ground that the nation is *unable to pay the interest in full?*'

It is painful to say that 'this thing' has gone on, and that 'the sweet simplicity of the Three per Cents' has given place to very much reduced interest. But one little ray of sunshine breaks on the gloomy picture. If Cobbett could ride this way once more he would discover that the acre of drying 'sheets, shirts, and other things' is no longer visible to shock the susceptibilities of old-fashioned wayfarers, or of that new feature of the road, the lady cyclist.

There is a great deal more of Cambridge Town, Camberley, and York Town now than when Cobbett last journeyed along the road: there are more 'children breeding up to be military commanders,' more Tommies, more drinking-shops, and an almost continuous line of ugly, and for the most part out-at-elbows, houses for a space of two miles. It is with relief that the traveller leaves behind the last of these wretched blots upon the country and descends into Blackwater, where the river of that name, so called from the sullen hue it obtains on running through the peaty wastes of this wild, heathy country, flows beneath a bridge at the entrance to the pretty village. Over this bridge we enter Hampshire, that county of hogs and chalky downs, but no sign of the chalk is reached yet, until coming upon the little stream in the level between Hartley Row and Hook, called the Whitewater from the milky tinge it has gained on coming down from the chalky heights of Alton and Odiham. This tinge is, however, more imaginary than real, and the characteristically chalky scenery of Hampshire is not seen by the traveller along the Great Western Road until Basingstoke and its chalk downs are reached.

Blackwater until recently possessed a picturesque old coaching inn, the 'White Hart,' which has unhappily been rebuilt. But it remains, as ever, a village of old inns. Climbing out of its one street we come to a wild and peculiarly unprepossessing tableland known as Hartford Bridge Flats.

To the lover of scenery this is a quite detestable piece of road, but the old coachmen simply revelled in it, for here was the best stretch of galloping ground in England, and they 'sprang' their horses over it for all they were worth, through Hartley Row and Hook, and well on towards Basingstoke.

The famous (or infamous let us rather call them) Hartford Bridge Flats are fully as dreary as any of the desolate Californian mining flats of which Bret Harte has written so eloquently. Salisbury Plain itself, save that the Plain is more extensive, is no worse place in which to be overtaken by bad weather. Excessively bleak and barren, the Flats are well named, for they stretch absolutely level for four miles: a black, open, unsheltered heath, with nothing but stunted gorse bushes for miles on either side, and the distant horizon closed in by the solemn battalions of sinister-looking pine-woods. The road runs, a straight and sandy strip, through the midst of this wilderness, unfenced, its monotony relieved only by a group of ragged firs about half-way. The cyclist who toils along these miles against a head wind is as unlikely to forget Hartford Bridge Flats as were the unfortunate 'outsides' on the coaches when rain or storm made the passage miserable.

Hartford Bridge, at the foot of the hill below this nightmare country, is a pretty hamlet of yellow sand and pine-woods, sand-martins and rabbits uncountable. The place is interesting and unspoiled, because its development was suddenly arrested when the Exeter Road became deserted for the railway in the early '40's; and so it remains, in essentials, a veritable old hamlet of the coaching days. Even more eloquent of old times is the long, long street of

Hartley Row which adjoins. Hartley Row was absolutely called into existence by the demand in the old days of road travel for stabling, inns, and refreshments, and is one of the most thoroughly representative of such roadside settlements. Half a mile to the south of the great highway is the parent village of Hartley Wintney, unknown to and undreamt of by travellers in those times, and probably much the

ROADSIDE SCENE (AFTER ROWLANDSON

same as it was in the Middle Ages. The well-named 'Row,' on the other hand, sprang up, grew lengthy, and flourished exceedingly during the sixty years of coaching prosperity, and then, at one stroke, was ruined. What Brayley, the historian of Surrey, wrote of Bagshot in 1841, applies even more eloquently to Hartley Row: 'Its trade has been entirely ruined by the opening of the Southampton and Great Western Railroads, and its numerous inns and public-houses, which had long been profitably occupied, are now almost destitute of business. Formerly thirty stage coaches passed through the village, now every coach has been taken off the road.' The 'Southampton Railroad,' referred to here, is of course the London and South-Western Railway, which has drained this part of the road of its traffic, and whose Winchfield station lies two miles away.

ROADSIDE SCENE (AFTER ROWLANDSON).

Before the crash of the '40's Hartley Row possessed a thriving industry in the manufacture of coaches, carried on by one Fagg, who was also landlord of the 'Bell Inn,' Holborn, and in addition horsed several stages out of London.

Some day the coming historian of the nineteenth century will, in his chapter on travel, cite Hartley Row as the typical coaching village, which was called into existence by coaching, lived on coaching, and with the death of coaching was stranded high and dry in this dried-up channel of life. All the houses of a village like this, which lived on the needs of travellers, faced the road in one long street, and almost every fourth or fifth house was an inn, or ministered in some way to the requirements of those who travelled. It is remarkable to find so many of these old inns still in existence at Hartley Row. Here they still stand, ruddy-faced, substantial but plain buildings, with, notwithstanding their plainness,

ROADSIDE SCENE (AFTER ROWLANDSON).

a certain air of distinction. The wayfarer, well read in the habits of the times when they were bustling with business, can imagine untold comforts behind those frontages; can reconstruct the scenes in the public waiting-rooms, where travellers, passing the interval between their being set down here by the 'Defiance' or the 'Regulator' Exeter coach and the arrival of the Odiham and Alton bye-stage, could warm themselves by the roaring fire; can sniff in imagination the coffee of the breakfasts and the roast beef of the dinners; or perceive through the old-fashioned window-frames the lordly posting parties, detained here by stress of weather, making the best of it by drinking of the old port or brown sherry which the cellars of every self-respecting coaching inn could then produce. Not that these were the only travellers familiar to the roadside village in those days. Not every one who fared from London to Exeter could afford the luxuries of the mail or stage coach, or of the good cheer and the lavender-scented beds just glimpsed. For the poor traveller there were the lumbering so-called 'Fly-vans' of Russell and Co., which jogged along at the average pace of three miles[1] an hour—the pace decreed by Scotland Yard for the modern policeman. The poor folk who travelled thus might perhaps have walked with greater advantage, 'save for the dignity of the thing,' as the Irishman said when the floor of his cab fell out and he was obliged to run along with the bottomless vehicle. Certainly they paid more for the misery of being conveyed thus than the railway traveller does nowadays for comfort at thirty to fifty miles an hour. Numbers *did* walk, including the soldiers and the sailors going to rejoin their regiments or their ships, who appear frequently in the roadside sketches of that period by Rowlandson and others. The poor travellers probably rode because of their—luggage I was about to write, let us more correctly say bundles.

When they arrived at a village at nightfall, they

[1] Waggons travelling at the rate of not more than four miles an hour were exempt from excise duty.

camped under the ample shelter of the great waggon; or, perhaps, if they had anything to squander on mere luxuries, spent sixpence or ninepence on a supper of cold boiled beef and bread, to be followed by a shake-down on straw or hay in the stable-lofts, which were quite commonly put to this use among the second- and third-rate inns of the old times.

Those were the days of the picturesque; if, indeed.

ROADSIDE SCENE. (AFTER ROWLANDSON.)

Rowlandson and Morland and the other delightfully romantic artists of the period did not invent those roadside scenes. Here, for instance, is Rowlandson's charming group of three old topers boozing outside the 'Half Moon.' I cannot tell you where this 'Half Moon' was. Probably the artist imagined it; but at anyrate the *kind* of place, and scenes of this description, must have existed in his time. Here, you will observe, the landlord has come out with a mug of 'humming ale' or 'nut-brown October' for the thirsty driver of the curricle, who is apparently going to market, if we may judge by the basket of fowls tied on to the back of the conveyance.

Scenes so picturesque as this are not to be observed in our own time, nor are the tramps who yet infest the road, singly or in families, of the engaging appearance of this family party. The human form divine was wondrously gnarled and twisted, or phenomenally fat, a hundred years ago, according to Rowlandson and Gillray. Legs like the trunks of contorted apple-trees, stomachs like terrestrial globes, mouths resembling the mouths of horses, and noses like geographical features on a large scale were the commonplaces of their practice, and this example forms no exception to the general rule.

XVII

The ruin that descended upon Hartley Row in common with other coaching towns and villages, nearly sixty years ago, has long since been lived down, and the long street, although quiet, has much the same cheerful appearance as it must have worn in the heyday of its prosperity. It is a very wide street, fit for the evolutions of many coaches. Pleasant strips of grass now occupy, more or less continuously, one side, and at the western end forks the road to Odiham, through a pretty common with the unusual feature of being planted with oak trees. These oak glades do not look particularly old; but, as it happens, we can ascertain their exact age and at the same time note how slow-growing is the oak tree by a reference to Cobbett's *Rural Rides*, where, in 1821, he notes their being planted: 'I perceive that they are planting oaks on the "*wastes*," as the *Agriculturasses* call them, about *Hartley Row*: which is very good, because the herbage, after the first year, is rather increased than diminished by the operation; while, in time, the oaks arrive at a timber state, and add to the beauty and the *real wealth* of the country, and to the real and solid wealth of the descendants of the planter who, in every such case, merits unequivocal praise, because he plants for his children's children. The planter here is Lady Mildmay, who is, it seems, Lady of the Manors about here.'

This planting was accomplished in days before any one so much as dreamt of the time to come, when the navies of the world should be built like tin kettles. Oaks were then planted with a view to being eventually worked up into the 'wooden walls of Old England,' among other uses, and the squires who laid out money on the work were animated by the glow of self-satisfaction that warms the breasts of those who can combine patriotism with the provision of a safe deferred investment. Unhappily, the 'wooden walls' have long since become a dim memory before these trees have attained their proper timber stage, and now stand, to those who read these facts, as monuments to blighted hopes. But they render this common extremely beautiful, and give it a character all its own. All this is quite apart from the legal aspect of the case; whether, that is to say, the lord of a manor has any right to make plantations of common lands for his own or his descendants' benefit. Cobbett, it will be perceived, calls these lands 'wastes,' following the term conferred upon them by the 'Agriculturasses'—whoever they may have been. If technically 'wastes of the manors,' then the landowner's right to do as he will is incontestable; but, with the contentious character of Cobbett before one, is it not remarkable that he should praise this planting and not question the right to call the land 'wastes,' instead of common? But perhaps Cobbett the tree-planter was contending with Cobbett the agitator, and the tree-planter got the best of it.

Hook, which succeeds Hartley Row, is a hamlet of the smallest size, but that fact does not prevent its possessing two old coaching inns, the 'White Hart' and the 'Old White Hart,' both very large and very near to one another. The Exeter Road certainly did not lack entertainment for man and beast in those days, with fine hostelries every few miles, either in the towns and villages, or else set down, solitary, amid the downs, like Winterslow Hut.

Nately Scures, whose second name is supposed to derive from the Anglo-Saxon *scora*, a shaw, or coppice (whence we get such place-names as Shawford, near Winchester: Shaugh Prior on Dartmoor; Shaw, in Berkshire, and many of the 'scors' forming the first syllables of place-names all over the country), is a place even smaller than Hook, with a tiny church, one of the many 'smallest' churches; standing in a meadow, to which access is had through rick-yards.

THE 'WHITE HART,' HOOK.

It is worth while halting a moment to gain a sight of the little church, which is late Norman, and one of the few dedicated to that Norman bishop, Saint Swithun.

Returning to the highway, and coming to the place known to the old coachmen as Mapledurwell Hatch, where that fine old coaching inn, the 'King's Head,' still stands, a road goes off to Old Basing, on the right, while the highway continues in a straight line, rising toward the town of Basingstoke.

The hasty traveller who knows nothing of the delights that await explorers in the byeways, misses a great deal here by keeping strictly to the high-road. If, instead of continuing direct to Basingstoke, this turning to the right hand is taken, it brings one in half a mile to the pretty village of Old Basing, celebrated for one of the most stubborn and protracted defences recorded in history. It was here that the equally crafty and courteous Sir William Paulet, first Marquis of Winchester, and Lord Treasurer during the reigns of Henry the Eighth, Edward the Sixth, Mary, and Elizabeth, built an immense palace on the site of Basing Castle. There can be little doubt that this magnificent person, who possessed no principles, and so kept place and power through the troublous times that these reigns comprised, must have had his hands in the Royal coffers to some purpose, or else have used his position for the sale of preferments. 'No oak, but an osier,' as his contemporaries said, he bowed before the tempests of religious persecution and the whirlwinds of conspiracies which passed him harmlessly by and left him still peculating. He had become a hoary-headed sinner by the time Elizabeth reigned, or there is no knowing but that he might have become a Prince Consort; for when he entertained Her Majesty here in 1560: 'By my troth,' said she, 'if my Lord Treasurer were but a young man, I could find it in my heart to have him for a husband before any man in England.' But she had said this kind of thing of many another.

The successors of this gorgeous nobleman—not being Lords Treasurers—could not afford to keep up so immense a palace, and so demolished a part of it, and found the remainder ample. To this place, fitting alike by its situation at a strategic point on the Western Road, and by the splendidly defensible nature of its site, crowded the King's Hampshire adherents who were not engaged at Winchester and Southampton at the outbreak of the war between Charles and his Parliament. John, fifth Marquis of Winchester, then ruled. '*Aimez Loyaulté*,' he wrote with his diamond ring on every window of his great mansion, and, provisioning his cellars, awaited events. As 'Loyalty' the house speedily became known to the flying bands of the King's men who, pursued through the country by the Roundheads, made for its shelter as birds do for trees in a storm. The rebels might hold Basingstoke for a time, and lay siege to Basing House, but troops from Royalist Oxford would come and take the town and reprovision this stronghold. It was a mixed company in this palace-fortress. My lord, loyalist, soldier, amateur of the arts; reposing after the warlike fatigues of the day in a bed whose gorgeous trappings made it worth £1300; witty and brave cavaliers: a company of Roman Catholic priests; men-at-arms, drinking, dicing, and fighting by turns and with equal zest: and such representatives of the arts as Inigo Jones, the architect, and Hollar, the engraver. Gay and careless though they were, they fought well, and slew and were slain to the number of two thousand during this long siege. Sometimes this varied garrison was hard pressed for food, when relief would come in whimsical fashion, as when Colonel Gage and his thousand horsemen appeared with sword in one hand and holding on to a bag of provisions with the other: a fitting contrast with the typical Puritan, a Psalm-book in his left hand and a pike in his right. Basing House, indeed, in the words of Carlyle, 'long infested the Parliament in these quarters, and was an especial eye-sorrow to the trade of London with the Western parts. It stood siege after siege for four years, ruining poor Colonel This and then poor Colonel That, till the jubilant Royalists had given it the name of *Basting* House.'

But the end was at hand after Fairfax had reduced the garrisons in the West and the Parliamentary troops could be spared from other places. Cromwell himself was charged with the business of taking 'Loyalty.' It was in September that he came to Basingstoke with horse and foot, and established a post of observation on the summit of Winklebury, a hill crowned with prehistoric earthworks that overlooks Worting and the Exeter Road, two miles on the other side of the town.

Little over a fortnight later Cromwell wrote that 'Thank God he was able to give a good account of Basing.' The house was taken by storm on the 14th October, 'while the garrison was card-playing,' as the persistent Hampshire legend would have us believe. 'Clubs are trumps, as when Basing House was taken,' is still an expression often heard at Hampshire card-parties, and some colour is lent to this story by the poor defence with which the furious onrush of Cromwell's troops was met. The attacking force lost few men, but a hundred of the defenders were killed, and three hundred more taken prisoners. Then the place caught fire and was utterly burnt, many perishing miserably in the great brick vaults of the house, where they were when the fire reached them. Fuller, that quaint seventeenth-century historian, who had been staying here, had, fortunately, left before the arrival of Cromwell's expedition. The continual fighting and the booming of the guns had distracted his attention from his work! There were others not so fortunate. Thomas Johnson, a peaceful botanist, was killed, and one Robinson, an actor and unarmed, was slaughtered by Harrison, the fanatic. 'Cursed is he that doeth the Lord's work negligently,' exclaimed the Puritan, as he cut him down. Other soldiers slew the daughter of Dr. Griffith who was charging them with being violent to her father.

Fanaticism and cupidity were fully satisfied on this occasion, save that there were those who grumbled because the lives of the Marquis of Winchester and his lieutenant were spared. The sack of Basing House yielded £200,000 worth of plunder, in objects

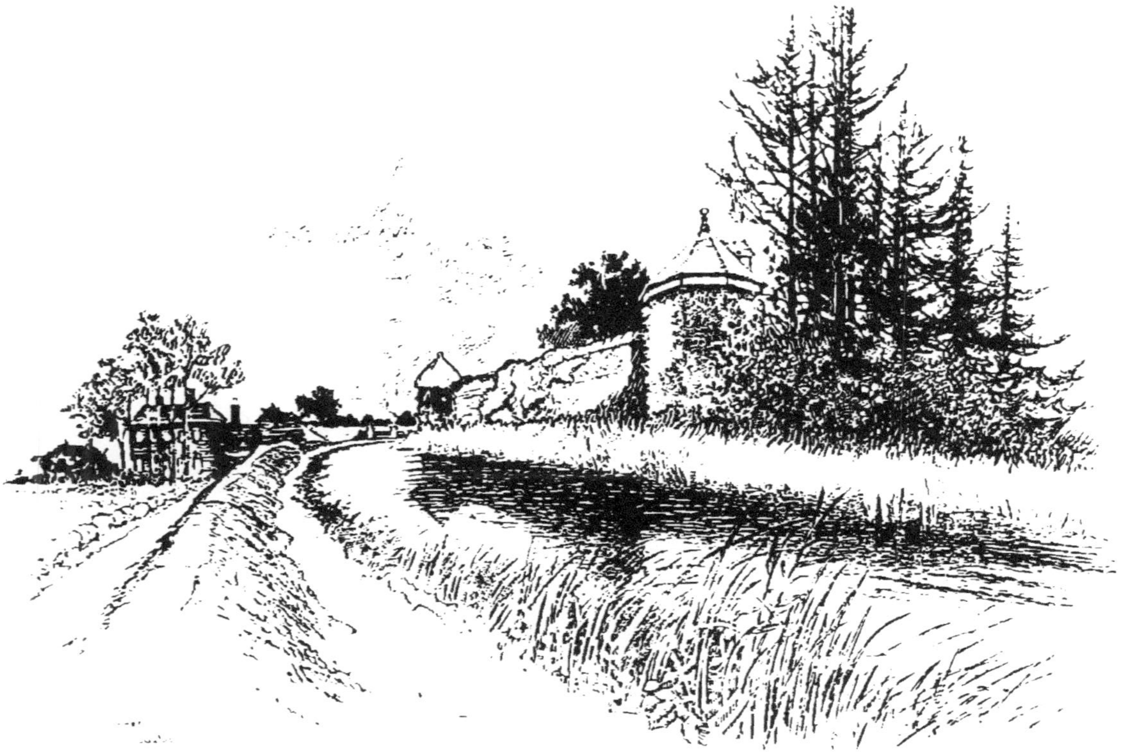

THE RUINS OF BASING HOUSE.

of art, gold and silver plate, coin, and provisions; and all partook of it, from Cromwell to the rank and file. 'One soldier had a hundred and twenty pieces of gold for his share, others plate, others jewels.' No wonder they had, with this dazzling prospect before them, rushed to the assault 'like a fire-flood.'

They made a rare business of this pillage, taking away the valuables, and selling the provisions to the country folks, who 'loaded many carts.' The bricks and building materials were given away, probably because they could not wait for the long business of selling them. 'Whoever will come for brick or stone shall freely have the same for his pains,' ran the proclamation, and, considering this, it is quite remarkable that even the existing scanty ruins of Basing House are left.

The area comprised within the defences measures fourteen and a half acres, now a tumbled and tangled stretch of ground, a mass of grassy mounds and hollows, overgrown in places with thickets. These ruins are entered from the road by an old brick gateway, still bearing the 'three swords in pile' on a shield, the arms of the Paulets, with ivy overhanging and tall trees behind. A tall curtain wall of brick, with a quaintly peaked-roofed tower at either end, now looks down upon the Basingstoke Canal, which many strangers think is the moat, but though a picturesque addition to the scene, it cannot claim any such historic associations, for it was only constructed close upon a hundred years ago.

Near by is Old Basing church, with square tower built of red brick, similar to that seen in the ruins of the House. It is said to be of foreign make. Bullets have up to recent years been extracted from the south door of the church, the original oak door in use two hundred and sixty years ago; and the flint and stone south walls and buttresses bear vivid witness, in their patching of brick, to the ruin that befell this part of the building in those troubled times. Strange to say, a beautiful group of the Virgin and Child still occupies a tabernacle over the west window, uninjured, although it can scarce have escaped the notice of the fanatical soldiery. Within the church are memorials of the loyal Paulets, Marquises of Winchester, and for a period Dukes of Bolton. Their glory has departed with their great House, and although a smaller residence was built in the meadows, close at hand, that has vanished too.

When Basing House was laid in ruins the Marquis of Winchester retired to his hunting lodge of Hawk Wood, to the south of Basingstoke, and, enlarging it, made the place his residence. His son, created Duke of Bolton, employed Inigo Jones to build a new house on the site of the lodge, and this is the present Hackwood Park. The existing house stands in the midst of dense and tangled woodlands, and although imposing, is a somewhat gloomy pile, with a ghost story. That bitter lawyer, Richard Bethell, of whom it was said that he 'dismissed Hell, with costs, and took away from orthodox members of the Church of England their last hope of everlasting damnation,' when he became Lord Chancellor and was created Baron Westbury, purchased Hackwood Park, and it was to one of his friends that the 'Grey Lady' of the mansion presented herself. Lord Westbury and a party of his friends had arrived from town soon after the purchase, and at a late hour they retired to rest, saying good-night to one another in the corridor. One of the guests woke up in the middle of the night and found his room strangely illuminated, with the indistinct outlines of a human figure visible in the midst of the uncanny glow. Thinking this some practical joke, and feeling very drowsy, he turned round and fell off to sleep again, to wake at a later hour and see the figure of a woman in a long, old-fashioned dress. With more courage than most people would probably have shown under the circumstances, he, instead of putting his head under the bed-clothes, jumped out, whereupon the lady modestly retired. Instead of going to bed again, he sat down and wrote an account of the occurrence; but when at breakfast Lord Westbury and his other friends kept continually asking him how he had slept, his suspicions as to a practical joke having been played upon him were renewed. He accordingly parried all these queries and said he had slept excellently, until Lord Westbury said, 'Now, look here, we saw that lady dressed in grey follow you into your room last night, you know!' Explanations followed, but the story of the 'Grey Lady' remains mysterious to this day.

The whereabouts of Basingstoke may be noted from afar by the huge and odd-looking clock-tower of the Town Hall, added to that building in 1887. Its windy height, visible from many miles around, is also favourable to the hearing at a distance of its sweet-toned carillons, modelled on the pattern of the famous peal of Bruges. When the shrieking of the locomotives at the railway station is hushed, and the wind is favourable, you may hear those tuneful bells far away over the melancholy wolds that hem in Basingstoke to the north and west, or listen to them by the waters of the Loddon eastward, or the undulating farm-lands of the south.

We have seen how Old Basing became of prime military importance from its situation at the point where many roads from the south and west of England converged and fell into one great highway to London; and from the same cause is due the commercial prosperity of Basingstoke. Basingstoke, with a record as a town going back to the time when the Domesday Book was compiled, is yet a mere modern settlement compared with the mother-parish of Old Basing; but it was an important place in the sixteenth century, when silks and woollens were manufactured here. At later periods this junction of the roads brought a great coaching trade, and has finally made Basingstoke a railway junction. Silks and woollens have given place to engineering works and machine-shops, and the town, with its modern reputation for the manufacture of agricultural machinery, bids fair at no distant date to become to Hampshire what Colchester and Ipswich are to Essex and Suffolk.

When the Parliamentary Generals were engaged in the long business of besieging Basing House, it may well be supposed that the town suffered greatly at the hands of their soldiery. They, who were experts at wrecking churches and cathedrals in a few hours, had ample opportunities for destruction in the four years that business was about. Their handiwork may be seen to this day—together with that of modern Toms, Dicks, and Harrys, who have not the excuse of being fanatics—in the ruined walls of Holy Ghost Chapel on the northern outskirts of the town. Within the roofless walls of the chapel, unroofed by those Roundheads for the sake of their leaden covering, are two recumbent effigies, sadly mutilated. Perhaps Sergeant Humility-before-the-Lord Mawworm slashed them with his pike in his hatred of worldly pomp; but his zeal did not do the damage wrought on the marble by the recording penknives of the past fifty years. A stained-glass window, pieced together from the fragments of those destroyed here, is still to be seen in Basingstoke Parish Church.

The Exeter Road leaves Basingstoke at its south-western end, where a fork of the highway gives a choice to the traveller of continuing to Andover on the right, or making on the left to Winchester. The first village on the way to Exeter is Worting, below the shoulder of Battle Down, a village—nay, a hamlet, let us call it—of a Sundayfied stillness.

Yet Worting has had its bustling times, for here was one of the most famous coaching inns on the road, the 'White Hart.' Another 'White Hart,' at Whitchurch, is scarcely less celebrated in the annals of the road. In fact, the 'White Harts' are so many and so notable on this road that the historian of the highways becomes almost as ashamed of mentioning them as of recounting the places which Cromwell stormed, or where Charles the Second hid; the houses in which Queen Elizabeth slept, or the inns where Pepys made merry.

Worting is followed in quick succession by the outskirts of Oakley, Clerken Green, Deane, Ashe, and Overton. Except Overton, which is a picturesque village lining the road, of the old coaching, or 'thoroughfare' type, these places are all shy and retiring, tucked away up bye-lanes, with great parks on their borders, in whose midst are very vast, very hideous country mansions where dwell the local J.P.'s, like so many Rogers de Coverley in miniature, with churches rebuilt or restored to their glory and the glory of God, and a general air of patronage bestowed upon the villagers and wayfarers from the outside world by those august partners. These parks, with their mile after mile of palings bordering the road, and their dense foliage overhanging it, are given over to solitude. An occasional gamekeeper, or a much more than occasional rabbit or hare, are the only signs of life, with perhaps the hoarse 'crock' of a pheasant's call from the neighbouring coverts. The air beneath the overarching trees along the road is stale and stagnant, and typical of the life here, like the green damp on the entrance lodges of Hall Place, where heraldic lions, sitting on their rumps and holding what at a distance look like quart-pots from the country inn opposite, scowl at one another across the gravelled drive.

It is a relief to emerge from this stifling atmosphere upon the open road where Overton stands. We are fully entered here into the valley of the Test, or Anton, a sparkling little stream whose course we follow henceforward as far as Hurstbourne Priors. Fishermen love Overton and this valley well, for there is royal sport here among the trout and grayling, and in the village a choice of those old inns which the angler appreciates as much as any one. Picturesque Overton is a doubly ruined village, for it has lost its silk industry, together with the coaching interest: but like the splendid bankrupts of modern high finance who fail for millions and continue to live like princes, it continues cheerful. Perhaps every one in the place made a competency before the crash, and put it away where no one could touch it!

The valley broadens out delightfully beyond Overton, and the road, reaching Laverstoke, commands beautiful views over the water-meadows, and the open park in whose midst stands Laverstoke House, clearly seen in passing. In this village, in the neat and clean paper-mill by the road, is made the paper for Bank of England notes. It was so far back as 1719 that this industry was established here by the Portal family, French Protestants emigrating from their country for conscience' sake. Cobbett, who hated paper-money as much as he did the 'Wen' in which it is chiefly current, passed this spot in a fury. He says, with a sad lack of the prophetic faculty, 'We passed the mill where the Mother-Bank paper is made! Thank God! this mill is likely soon to want employment. Hard by is a pretty park and house, belonging to "'*Squire*" Portal, the *paper-maker*. The country people, who seldom want for sarcastic shrewdness, call it "Rag Hall!"' And again, 'I hope the time will come when a monument will be erected where that mill stands, and when on that monument will be inscribed "*the Curse of England*." This spot ought to be held accursed in all time henceforth and for evermore. It has been the spot from which have sprung more and greater mischief than ever plagued mankind before.'

Unhappily for Cobbett's wishes and predictions, the mill is still in existence and is busier than it was when he wrote in 1821. There are as many as two hundred and fifty people now employed here in the making of the 'accursed' paper.

Now comes Freefolk village, with a wayside drinking-fountain and a tall cross, with stone seat, furnished with some pious inscription; the whole erected by a Portal in 1870, and intended to further the honour and glory of that family. There is plenty water everywhere around, in the river and its many runlets amid the water-meadows, but the fountain is dry. Passing tramps are properly sarcastic, and the dry fountain and its texts, so far from leading in the paths of temperance and godliness, are the occasion of much blasphemy. But the pious Portals have their advertisement.

Whitchurch, two miles down the road, is approached past the much-quarried hills that rise on the right hand and shelter that decayed little town from the buffetings of the north-easterly winds. If there be those who are curious to learn what a decayed old coaching town is like, let them journey to Whitchurch. After much tiresome railway travelling, and changing at junctions, they will arrive in the fulness of time at Whitchurch station, whence the omnibus of the 'White Hart' will drive them, rumbling over the stone-pitched streets of the town, to the door of that quaint inn, in one of whose rooms the future Cardinal Newman wrote the beginning of the *Lyra Apostolica*:—

Are these the tracks of some unearthly friend?

2nd December 1832, while waiting for the mail to Falmouth. He had come from Oxford that morning by the Oxford-Southampton coach.

'Here I am,' he says, writing to his mother, 'from one till eleven,' waiting for the down Exeter mail. Think, modern railway traveller, what would you say were it your lot to wait ten hours, say at Templecombe Junction, for a connection! Moreover, a bore claiming to be the brother of an acquaintance claimed to share his room and his society at the 'White Hart,' and eventually journeyed to Exeter with him. The future Cardinal did not like this. He writes: 'I am practising for the first time the duty of a traveller, which is sorely against the grain, and have been talkative and agreeable without end,' adding (one can almost imagine the sigh of the retiring scholar!), 'Now that I have set up for a man of the world, it is my vocation.'

The latter part of his journey was accomplished at night. Travelling thus through Devonshire and Cornwall is, he remarks, 'very striking for its mysteriousness.' It was a beautiful night, 'clear, frosty, and bright, with a full moon. Mere richness of vegetation is lost by night, but bold features remain. As I came along, I had the whole train of pictures so vividly upon my mind that I could have written a most interesting account of it in the most approved picturesque style of modern composition, but it has all gone from me now, like a dream.

'The night was enlivened by what Herodotus calls a "night engagement" with a man, called by courtesy a gentleman, on the box. The first act ended by his calling me a d—d fool. The second by his insisting on two most hearty shakes of the hand, with the protest that he certainly did think me very injudicious and ill-timed. I had opened by telling him he was talking great nonsense to a silly goose of a maid-servant stuck atop of the coach; so I had no reason to complain of his giving me the retort uncourteous.'

There are corridors in the 'White Hart' with up and down twilight passages, in which the guests of another day lost themselves with promptitude and despatch. There is also a barbarically coloured coffee-room, snug and comfortable, which looks as though Washington Irving could have written an eloquent essay around it; and, more essential than anything else in days of old, a capacious yard with huge yawning stables. For Whitchurch is at the cross

WHITCHURCH

roads, along which in one direction went the Exeter mails, while at right angles goes the road between Southampton, Winchester, Newbury, Didcot, and Oxford, little used now, but once an important route. Whitchurch, in the gay old times when few men had votes but every voter had his price, used to send two members to Parliament. Horrid Reform and Bribery Acts which, together with the extension of the franchise and the adoption of secret voting, have brought about the disfranchising of rotten boroughs and the decay of such home industries as electoral corruption, personation, and the like, have taken away much of the prosperity of the town, which, like Andover, used to live royally from one election to another on the venality of the 'free and independent.' But the last visit of the 'Man in the Moon' was paid to Whitchurch very many years ago, and not even the oldest inhabitant can recollect the days when cash was given for votes and the electors, gloriously and incapably drunk, were herded together to plump for the candidate with the longest purse.

When it is said that Whitchurch is a tiny town of very steep, narrow, and crooked streets, that it still boasts some vestiges of its old silk industry, and that it is a 'Borough by prescription,' all its salient points have been exhausted. Reform has not only reformed away the Parliamentary representation of the town, but has also swept away the municipal authority. Mayor and bailiff are both elected every year, but the offices carry no power nowadays.

Leaving Whitchurch, the road presently comes to the village of Hurstbourne Priors, which stands in a hollow on the Bourne, an affluent of the Anton, and on the verge of the Ancient and Royal Forest of Harewood. Not only does the village stand on the banks of the stream and the edge of the woods, but it also derives the first of its two names from these circumstances, 'Hurstbourne' being obviously descriptive of woodlands and brooklet, while the 'Priors' is a relic of its old lords of the manor, the abbots of Saint Swithun's at Winchester. These historic and geographical facts, however, are apt to be lost in the local corruption of the place-name, and that of Hurstbourne Tarrant, a few miles higher up the stream; for they are, according to Hampshire speech, respectively 'Up Husband' and 'Down Husband.'

XIX

The road between this point and Andover, ascending the high ground between the Ann and the Test, is utterly without interest, and brings the traveller down into the town at the south side of the market square without any inducement to linger on the way. Except on the Saturday market-day, Andover is given over to a dreamy quiet. The butchers' dogs lie blinking sleepily on the thresholds, or on the kerbs, and regard with a pained surprise, rather than with any active resentment, the intrusive passage of a stray customer. Tradesmen's assistants leisurely open casual crates of goods on the pavements, with long intervals for gossip between the drawing of each nail, and no one objects to the blocking of the footpath. A chance cyclist manœuvres in the empty void of the road in the midst of the square, and collides with no one, for the simple reason that there is nobody to collide with, and one acquaintance talks to another across the wide space and is distinctly heard. Formal but not unpleasing houses front on to this square, together with the usual Town Hall, and a great modern, highly uninteresting Gothic church, erected after the model of Salisbury Cathedral, on the site of the old building.

For fifty-one weeks of the fifty-two that comprise the year, this is the weekly six-days aspect of the place, varied occasionally by the advent of a travelling circus, or the arrival of a route-marching detachment of the Royal Artillery, who park their guns in the square, and may be seen in the stable-yards of the inns on which they are billeted, in various stages of dishevelment, in shirt-sleeves rolled up to elbows, and braces dangling at waists, littering down their horses, or smoking very short and very foul pipes.

All this idyllic quiet is blown to the winds during the week of Weyhill Fair, the October pandemonium held three and a half miles away. Then hordes of cattle- and horse-jobbers, hop growers and buyers, cheese-factors, and the travellers of firms dealing in machinery, seeds, oil-cake, tarpaulins, and half a hundred other everyday agricultural requisites, descend upon the town. Then are dragged out from mysterious receptacles the most antiquated of 'flys,' and waggonettes, and nondescript vehicles, to be pressed into the service of conveying visitors to the

Fair, some three and a half miles from the town. Whence they come, and where they are hidden away afterwards, is more than the stranger can tell, but it is quite certain that their retreat is in some corner where spiders dwell, and earwigs and other weird insects have a home. Add to these facts the all-important one that it is generally possible to walk the distance in a shorter time, and you have a full portraiture of the average Weyhill conveyance.

This sleepy old place, older by many more centuries than the oldest house remaining here can give any hint of, was not always so quiet. There were alarums and excursions (ending, however, with not so much as a cut finger) when James the Second, falling back from Salisbury before the advance of his son-in-law, William of Orange, halted here. There might have been a battle in Andover's streets, or under the shadow of Bury Hill, had James put a bolder front on the business; but instead of cutting up William's Dutchmen, he just dined overnight, and hearing in the morning that his other son-in-law, Prince George of Denmark, had slunk off with Lords Ormond and Drumlanrig, went off himself, strategically to the rear. He was an obstinate and ridiculous bigot, and a quite unlovable monarch, but he had a power of sarcasm. 'What,' said he, hearing of the Prince's desertion, and bitterly mimicking the absurd intonation of that recreant's French catch-phrase, 'is "*Est-il possible?*" gone too? Truly, a good trooper would have been a greater loss.'

After these events, that era of bribery and corruption set in, which is mistakenly supposed to have been brought to an end through the agency of the several Reform Acts, passed by well-meaning Legislatures to secure the purity of Parliamentary elections. As if treating, and the crossing of horny hands with gold were the only ways of corrupting a constituency that the wit of man, or the address of a candidate, could discover! The palm no longer receives the coin; but who has not heard of the modern art of 'nursing a constituency,' by which the candidate, eager for Parliamentary honours, sits down before a town, or a county division, subscribes liberally to hospitals and horticultural societies, cricket and football clubs, opens bazaars, and presides at Young Men's Christian Associations, thereby winning the votes which would in other days have been acquired by palming the men and kissing all the babies? This tea-fight business gives us no picturesque situations like that in which Charles James Fox figured. Fox was canvassing personally, and called upon one of the bluff and blunt order of voters, who listened to his eloquence, and remarked, 'Sir, I admire your abilities, but damn your principles!' To which Fox supplied the obvious retort, 'Sir, I admire your sincerity, but damn your manners!'

Andover no longer sends a representative to Parliament, but in the brave old days it elected two. With a knowledge of the wholesale purchasing of votes that then went on, it will readily be perceived that Andover, with two members to elect, must have been a place flowing with milk and honey; or, less metaphorically, a happy hunting-ground for guineas and free drinks. It was somewhere about a hundred and fifty years ago that Sir Francis Blake Delaval, a prominent rake and practical humorist of the period, was canvassing Andover. One voter amid the venal herd was, to all appearance, proof against all temptations. Money, wine, place, flattery had no seductions for this stoic. The baffled candidate was beside himself in his endeavours to discover the man's weak point; for of course it was an age in which votes were so openly bought and sold that the saying 'Every man has his price' was implicitly believed. Only what *was* this particular voter's figure? Strange to say, he had no weakness for money, but was possessed with an inordinate desire to see a fire-eater, and doubted if there existed people endowed with that remarkable power. 'Off went Delaval to London, and returned with Angelo in a post-chaise. Angelo exerted all his genius. Fire poured from his mouth and nostrils—fire which melted that iron nature, and sent it off cheerfully to poll for Delaval!'

This was that same Delaval whose attorney sent him the following bill of costs after one of his contests:—

> To being thrown out of the window of the George Inn, Andover; to my leg being thereby broken; to surgeon's bill, and loss of time and business; all in the service of Sir Francis Delaval, £500.

And cheap too.

They kept this sort of thing up for many years; not always, however, throwing solicitors out of hotel windows; although rival political factions often expressed their determination to throw one another's candidate in the Anton, after the fashion of the bills posted in the town during a contest in the '40's, which announced in displayed type—

LORD HUNTINGTOWER FOR EVER!

SIR JOHN POLLEN IN THE RIVER!!

CATCHING FISH FOR HIS LORDSHIP'S DINNER!!!

History does not satisfy us on the point whether or not those furious partisans carried out their threat; or whether, if they did, their victim afforded good bait.

This Lord Huntingtower was the eldest son of the late Earl of Dysart, and a well-matched companion of the late Marquis of Waterford. Roaming the country-side on dark nights, mounted on stilts, with sheets over their clothes and hollowed turnips on their heads with scooped-out holes for eyes and mouth, and lit with candles, they frightened many a timid rustic out of his dull wits. In daytime they played practical jokes on the tradesfolk of Andover. For example, entering a little general shop in the town, Lord Huntingtower asked for a pound of treacle. 'Where shall I put it?' asked the old woman who kept the shop, seeing that the usual basin was not forthcoming.

'P-pup-pup-put it in my hat,' said my Lord, who stuttered in yard-lengths, holding out his 'topper.' The pound of treacle was accordingly poured into the Lincoln and Bennett, and the next instant it was on the shopkeeper's head.

This was the manner in which Lord Huntingtower endeared himself to the people—those, that is to say, who were not the victims of his pleasantries.

That kind of person is quite extinct now. They should have (but unfortunately they have not) a stuffed specimen in the Natural History Museum at South Kensington; because he is numbered with the Dodo, the Plesiosaurus, and the Mastodon. The Marquis of Winchester who flourished at the same period as my Lords Huntingtower and Waterford was of the same stamp. He had the fiery Port Countenance which was the sign of the three-bottle man, and his life and the deeds that he did are still fondly remembered at Andover, for his country-house was at Amport, in the immediate neighbourhood. He was the Premier Marquis of England, and although up to his neck in mortgages and writs, an extremely Great Personage. Let us, therefore, take our hats off as humbly as we know how to do.

When he was at his country-place he worshipped at the little village church of Amport. Sometimes he did not worship, but slept, lulled off to the Land of Nod by the roaring fire he kept in his room-like pew. On one occasion it chanced that he was wide awake, and, like the illustrious Sir Roger de Coverley, leant upon the door of that pew, and gazed around to satisfy himself that all his tenantry were present. Then an awful thing happened, the hinges of the door broke, and it fell with a great clatter to the ground, and the Marquis with it. He said 'Damn!' with great fervour and unction, and everybody laughed. No one thought it—as they should have done—shocking, which shows the depravity of the age.

There is no doubt whatever about that depravity, which, like the worm in the bud, has wrought ruin among our manners since then. How sad it is that we are not now content to call upon Providence to

> Bless the squire and his relations
> And keep us in our proper stations;

but are all too intent upon 'getting on,' to defer to rank, or take a spell at the delightful occupations of tuft-hunting and boot-licking! Even in those days this horrid decadence had begun to manifest itself, as you will see by the story of this same Marquis and Mr. Assheton Smith of Tedworth Park. Mr. Smith could (as the saying goes) have 'bought up' the impoverished Marquis of Winchester several times over, and not have felt any strain upon his resources. Moreover, he was a Squire of great consideration in these parts, and as Master of the Tedworth Hunt, something of a rival in importance. For which things, and more, the Marquis hated him, and on one occasion took an opportunity of reproving him publicly before the whole field, in the fine florid language of which he had so ready a command. Possibly Mr. Smith had committed the unpardonable indignity of showing my lord the way over a particularly stiff fence he was hesitating at. At any rate the language of the Premier Marquis was violent, and contained some reference to the disparity between their respective ranks. But the Squire was ready with his retort. He said, 'Anyhow, I'd sooner be a rich Squire than a poor Marquis!' The field smiled, because the reduced circumstances of the Marquis of Winchester had been notorious ever since his father had been secretly buried at midnight in the family vault at Amport, for fear the bailiffs should seize the body for debt.

There are, for good or ill, no such sportsmen nowadays as there were in the times before railways came and brought more competition into existence, making life a business and a struggle, instead of the light-hearted and irresponsible game that the sporting squires at least found it. Noble sportsmen do not nowadays, when detained by stress of weather in a country inn, while away the tedium of the afternoon by backing the raindrops racing down the window-panes and betting fortunes on the result. No, that very real bogey, 'agricultural depression,' has stopped that kind of full-blooded prank, and the titled in these progressive times find their account on the 'front page' of company-promoters' swindles instead. They barter good names for gold, and lick the boots of wealthy rogues, instead of kicking their bodies. Where their fathers scorned to go the sons delight to be. Would the fathers have done the like had 'agricultural depression' come earlier?

The noblemen and the sporting squires of old lived in one mad whirl of excitement. They gambled on every incident in their lives, and sometimes even on their death-beds; like the old gamester who, when the doctor told him he would be dead the next morning, offered to bet him that he would not! We are not told whether or not the medical man backed his professional opinion.

One of the most illuminating side-lights on these truly Corinthian folk is the story which tells how Lord Albert Conyngham and that classic sportsman,

Mr. George Payne, were travelling from London to Poole by post-chaise in the last decade of the coaching days—that is to say, between 1830 and 1840. They found the journey tedious, and so played écarté, in which they grew so interested that they continued playing all day and into the night, the chaise being lit with the aid of a patent lamp which Mr. Payne always took with him on a long journey. The play was high; £100 a game, with bets on knaves and sequences, and had been continued with varying success, until when they were passing in the darkness of night through the New Forest, Mr. Payne, who had been a heavy loser for some time, had a run of luck. In midst of this exciting play the post-boy, who, in the secluded glades of the Forest, had managed to lose the road, stopped the chaise and, dismounting, tapped at the window. But so engrossed were the two travellers in the cards that they had not noticed that the conveyance was standing still, and the post-boy stood tapping there for a long while before he was heard.

'What on earth do you want?' angrily asked the winning gambler, indignant at this interruption.

'Please, sir,' replied the post-boy, 'I've lost my way.'

'Then,' rejoined Mr. Payne, pulling up the window with a bang, 'come and tell us when you've found it, and be damned to you!'

XX

Cobbett, that sturdy Radical and consistent grumbler, had an adventure at Andover, at the 'George Inn.' It was in October 1826, on returning from Weyhill Fair, that he took occasion to dine here. Of course he had no business or pleasure at the 'George,' for he had secured a lodging elsewhere; but with that obsession of his for agitation he must needs repair to the inn and dine at the ordinary; less we may be sure for the sake of the meal than to embrace the opportunity of addressing the farmers, the cattle-dealers, cheese and hop factors, and bankers whom he knew would be dining there at Fair-time. It was an opportunity not to be missed.

He must have been sadly disappointed at first, for there were only about ten people dining; but when it was seen that this was the well-known Cobbett, the diners increased, and, after the meal was over, the room became inconveniently crowded; guests coming from other inns until at length the room door was left open so that the crowd in the passage and on the stairs, which were crammed from top to bottom, might listen to the inevitable harangue on the sins of kings, and governments, and of landowners, and the criminal stupidity of every one else.

At this stage of the proceedings, just as the dinner was done, one of the two friends by whom he was accompanied gave Cobbett's health. This, naïvely adds the arch-agitator, 'was of course followed by a *speech*; and, as the reader will readily suppose, to have an opportunity of making a speech was the main motive for my going to dine at *an inn*, at any hour. and especially at *seven o'clock* at night.' That, at any rate, is frank enough.

After he had been thus holding forth on ruin, past, present, and to come, for half an hour or so, it seems to have occurred to the landlord that the company upstairs were drinking very little for so large a concourse, and he accordingly forced his way through the crowd, up the staircase, and along the passage into the dining-room. Cobbett had already cast an unfavourable eye upon that licensed victualler, and describes him as 'one Sutton, a rich old fellow, who wore a round-skirted sleeved fustian waistcoat, with a dirty white apron tied round his middle, and with no coat on; having a look the *eagerest* and the *sharpest* that I ever saw in any set of features in my whole lifetime; having an air of authority and of mastership, which, to a stranger, as I was, seemed quite incompatible with the meanness of his dress and the vulgarity of his manners: and there being, visible to every beholder, constantly going on in him a pretty even contest between the servility of avarice and the insolence of wealth.'

The person who called forth this severe description having forced his way into the room, some one called out that he was causing an interruption, to which he replied that that was, in fact, what he had come to do, because all this speechifying injured the sale of his liquor! Can it be doubted that this roused all the lion in Cobbett's breast? He first of all tells us that 'the disgust and abhorrence which such conduct could not fail to excite produced, at first, a desire to quit the room and the house, and even a proposition to that effect. But, after a minute or so, to reflect, the company resolved not to quit the room, but to turn him out of it who had caused the interruption; and the old fellow, finding himself *tackled*, saved the labour of shoving, or kicking, him out of the room, by retreating out of the doorway, with all the activity of which he was master.'

The speech at last finished, the company began to settle down to what Cobbett calls the 'real business of the evening, namely, drinking, smoking, and singing.' It was a Saturday night, and as there was all the Sunday morning to sleep in, and as the wives of the company were at a convenient distance, the circumstances were favourable to an extensive consumption of 'neat' and 'genuine' liquors. At this juncture the landlord announced, through the waiter, that he declined to serve anything so long as Mr. Cobbett remained in the room! This uncorked all the vials of wrath of which Cobbett had so large and bitter a supply. 'Gentlemen,' he said, 'born and bred, as you know I was, on the borders of this county, and fond as I am of bacon, Hampshire hogs have with me always been objects of admiration rather than of contempt; but that which has just happened here induces me to observe that this feeling of mine has been confined to hogs of four legs. For my part, I like your company too well to quit it. I have paid this fellow six shillings for the wing of a fowl, a bit of bread, and a pint of small beer. I have a right to sit here; I want no drink, and those who do, being refused it here, have a right to send to other houses for it, and to drink it here.'

Mine host, alarmed at this declaration of independence, withdrew the prohibition, and indeed brought up pipes, tobacco, and the desired drinks himself; and soon after this entered the room with two gentlemen who had inquired for Mr. Cobbett, and laying his hand on Cobbett's knee, smiled and said the gentlemen wished to be introduced. 'Take away your paw,' thundered the agitator, shaking the strangers by the hand; 'I am happy to see you, even though introduced by this fellow.' After which they all indulged in the English equivalent of the Scotch 'willie waucht' until half-past two in the morning.

'But,' remarks Cobbett, as a parting shot, 'the next time this old sharp-looking fellow gets *six shillings* from me for a dinner, he shall, if he choose, *cook me*, in any manner that he likes, and season me with hand so unsparing as to produce in the feeders thirst unquenchable.'

XXI

Weyhill Fair, which brought Cobbett and the people he harangued into Andover, is a thoroughly old English institution, and although the old custom of fairs is gradually dying out, and this, the Largest Fair in England, is not so important as it was a hundred years ago, it is still a place where much money changes hands once a year. Weyhill is supposed to be one of the places mentioned in *Piers Plowman's Vision*, in the line:

> At Wy and at Wynchestre I went to ye fair,

and it is the 'Weydon Priors' of the *Mayor of Casterbridge*, where Henchard sells his wife.

Weyhill Fair was once—in the fine fat days of agricultural prosperity, when England was always at war with France, and corn was dear—a six-days fair. As the 'oldest inhabitant' to be discovered nowadays at Weyhill will complain, shaking his head sadly the while, 'There warn't none o' them 'ere 'sheenery fal-lals about in them days to do the wark o' men and harses so's no-one can't get no decent living like, d'ye see?' If by ''sheenery,' you understand mechanical appliances—'machinery,' in fact—to be meant, you will see how distrustfully the agricultural mind still marches to the modern quick-step of progress. There is always plenty of machinery on view at Weyhill Fair: ploughs and harrows, and such like inanimate things, and machinery in motion; steam threshers, winnowers, binders, and the like, threshing, and winnowing, and binding the empty air.

There are special days set apart—and more or less rigorously observed—for Hiring, for Pleasure, for the Hop Fair, and for the sale of sheep. This great annual fixture begins on Old Michaelmas Eve, 10th October, and lasts four days, as against the six days, that were all too short in which to do the business, up to fifty years ago. Railways have dealt the old English institution of fairs a deadly blow all over the country, and before many more years have gone the majority of them will be things of the past. Their reason for existing will then be quite gone, even as it is now going. Before railways came into being the farmer travelled little, and his men not at all. From one year's end to the other they probably never saw a town beyond their nearest marketing centre, and they certainly never made the acquaintance of London. So, since the farmer and his men, the mistress and her maids, could not get about to buy, it follows that those who had goods to sell had need to take all the advantage possible of that great and glorious institution, the Fair.

Bitterly disappointed in the old days were those who, from some reason or another, were prevented from coming to this Promised Land of gay and glittering stalls and booths. Jolly and convivial, on the other hand, were those who had the luck to be able to come. 'Oh, dear! what can the matter be? Johnny's so long at the Fair,' commences an old country song. We can guess pretty well what the matter was, just as certainly as if we had been there ourselves. Johnny, of course, had got too much cider, or strong, home-brewed October 'humming ale' into him, and, as the rustics would put it, 'couldn't stir a peg, were't ever so.' And so the girl he left behind him at the farmhouse had need of all the patience at her command while she waited for his return. She probably didn't much care—for Johnny's sake; rather for another reason. As thus:

He promised he'd buy me a fairing to please me;
A bunch of blue ribbons to tie up my bonny brown hair.

It was the blue ribbons she wanted, you see. Let us, dear friends, hope she got them.

Many dangers threatened the Johnnies—the Colin Clouts of that time. The fair was the happy hunting-ground of Sergeant Kite, who used to treat the dull-witted fellows until they were stupid as owls, when, *hey presto!* the Queen's Shilling was clapped into their nerveless palms, and they woke the next morning to find themselves duly enlisted, with a bunch of parti-coloured ribbons fixed in their hats as a token and badge of their military servitude. Then 'what price' those blue ribbons lying forgotten in the pocket for the disconsolate fair one? Nothing under a fine of twenty pounds sterling sufficed to release a recruit in those days, and as few families could then afford that ransom, the fair was a turning-point in the career of many a lusty fellow.

The recruiting sergeant still does a little business at Weyhill, but his claws are nowadays cut very close.

Weyhill, as you approach it, is situated, much to your surprise, not on a hill at all, but rather on the flat. It is a mere nothing of a village, and beyond the parish church, the inevitable inn, and the equally inevitable farmhouse, houses are very much to seek.

The stranger who happens upon the place at any other than fair time is astonished by the large numbers of open sheds and the numerous clusters of long, low, thatched, and white-washed cottages, situated on a wide, open, grassy common beside the road, all empty, and every one bearing boldly-painted announcements, in black paint, of 'Hot Dinners,'

'Refreshments,' and the like. The stranger might be excused if he thought this some bankrupt settlement whose vanished inhabitants, like the people of that mythical place who 'eked out a precarious existence by taking in one another's washing,' had lived on selling refreshments to each other until they had finally all died of indigestion. He would be very much mistaken, however, in his surmise, for this is Weyhill Fair-ground in undress. If you wish to see it in full swing, you must visit the spot between 10th and 13th October, when it is lively enough.

The first day is the Sheep Fair. As many as 150,000 sheep have been sold here on this day. The Horse Fair is held every day; and an astonishing number and variety of horses there are too. Irish horses, brought all the way from Cork, Scotch horses, Welsh horses; every kind of horse, from the Suffolk Punch to the New Forest Pony. Great lumbering young cart-horses stand behind their pens with manes and tails plaited to wonderment with straw, for all the world like beauties dressed for the County Ball, and just as proud and self-conscious. Do you want to buy a horse of any kind at the Fair? Then don't!—unless, indeed, you know all that is to be known about horses, and a bit over; otherwise the dealer will 'have' you, for a dead certainty. To see them showing off a horse's good qualities and hiding his bad ones is a liberal education, but see that you acquire your knowledge at some one else's expense. With this determination you can afford to be well amused with the waving of coloured flags on long sticks, by which the horses are made to pirouette before the eyes of likely purchasers, and can safely smile at the wily dealer's exclamations of 'There's blood!' 'Get up, my beauty!' and 'Here's the quality!'

The very pick of the horseflesh, however, does not reach Weyhill. The dealers bring their stock with them by road from Milford, Holyhead, Scotland, at the rate of ten miles a day, and as they thus have to come a hundred or a hundred and fifty miles, the journey takes from ten days to a fortnight. This would be a serious expense and loss of time were it not for the fact that dealers always look to make sales along the road.

The second day of the Fair is known as Mop Fair, or Molls' and Johns' Day. Its official title is the Hiring, or Statute Fair. At twelve o'clock, mid-day, farm-servants, men or women, 'Molls' or 'Johns,' leave their employ, and, drawing their wages, offer themselves to be hired for the coming twelvemonth. They stand in long lines, the carters with a length of plaited whipcord in their hats, the shepherds with a lock of wool, and wait while the farmers come and bargain with them. When they have struck up an agreement, the men proceed to fix coloured ribbons in their hats, and do their best to have a merry time with the wages they have just received.

There is certainly every opportunity of spending money on the spot. Steam merry-go-rounds keep up a continual screeching and bellowing; stalls with all manner of toys and nicknacks of the most grotesque shapes and hideous colouring; cake and sweetmeat stalls, loaded, as Weyhill stalls have been from time immemorial, with Salisbury gingerbread; Aunt

Sallies; try-your-strength machines, and a hundred others compete for the rustic's coin. Then, if he wants a new suit of clothes, here is the clothier's stall, where Hodge can bespeak a suit, wear it during the next twelve months, and pay for it next Fair, just as his father and grandfather used to do before him. All the booths visited, the horse medicines stall inspected, the latest improvements in agricultural machinery gaped at, Hodge repairs to the refreshment hovels, wherein certain crafty men who have come down for the occasion from London are awaiting him, to treat the unsuspecting yokel to drinks, to lure him on to play cards, and finally to cheat him and pick his pockets in the most finished and approved fashion. For these gentry, and for the disorderly in general, there is a police-station on the ground, with cells all complete, and with local magistrates every morning to hear cases, and to consign prisoners, if necessary, to Winchester Gaol, sixteen miles away.

The third and fourth days are now given up to the Pleasure and Hop Fairs. One of the smaller trades connected with the malting and general agricultural industries is that of malt-shovel and barn-shovel making. These are wooden shovels of a peculiar shape, and are sold only at one stall. Another of the minor businesses is that of umbrella selling. The umbrellas are very fine and large, and of a kind that would make a marked man of any Londoner who should use one in town.

The Cheese Fair is now a small one, dealings generally being confined to local folks, who delight in the Blackmore and 'Blue Vinney' cheeses of this and the adjoining counties. London dealers still attend the Hop Fair, in which many thousands of pounds' worth of hops change hands to the drinking of much champagne, brought on to the ground by the cart-load, as in the brave days of yore. There are two distinct hop markets, the Farnham Row and the Country Side. Hops from Farnham, Bentley, Petersfield, Liphook, and other neighbouring places find a ready market. They are sold more exclusively by sample than formerly, and so only a few 'pockets,' as the tightly packed sacks are named, are visible. Round them dealers may be seen, rubbing the hops in their hands and smelling them with a knowing look, while the vendor cuts another sample out of the pocket for the next likely customer. He does this with a singular steel instrument called a 'sample drawer.' First a sharp and long-bladed knife is thrust into the hard mass, and two sides cut, and then the broad-bladed 'drawer' driven in and screwed tight, bringing out a compact square of hops to be tested.

By nine o'clock every night all the booths and stalls have to be closed, and stillness reigns over the scene, save for the cough of the sheep, the occasional lowing of the cattle, or the fretful whinnying of a wakeful horse. And when the last day of the Fair is done, the booths are all shut up and deserted, and desolation reigns again for a year.

The trail of the Romans is over all the surroundings of Andover, and they must have loved this fishful and fertile valley well, for ample relics of extensive settlements and gorgeous villas have been unearthed by the plough. Some of the fine mosaic pavements discovered here are now in the British Museum, and every now and again the shepherd or the ploughman picks up a worn and battered coin of the Cæsars in the neighbouring fields. One of the finest Roman pavements came from the village of Abbot's Ann, a short distance away, under the shadow of the great bulk of Bury Hill, which, crowned with prehistoric earthworks of cyclopean size, frowns down upon the valley. The whimsical name of this village and that of Little Ann derive from the stream, the Ann, or Anton, on whose banks they are situated.

In this village of Abbot's Ann there still prevails a remarkable custom. On the death of a young unmarried person of the parish, his or her friends and relatives make a funeral garland, or chaplet, similar to the one sketched overleaf, in paper, and hang it from the ceiling of the church. The interior of the building now holds quite a number of these singular mementoes, the oldest dating back to the last century. They are fashioned of cardboard and white paper, something in the shape of a crown, with elaborately cut rosettes and with five paper gloves suspended, on two of which are recorded the name, the age, and the date of death of the deceased whose memory is thus kept alive, while the other three are inscribed with texts or verses from favourite hymns. The particulars of age and death are repeated on a little wooden shield above.

During the last eight years three of these memorials have been added. They are placed here after having been carried in front of the coffin on the day of the funeral. On such occasions the garland is carried by two girls, dressed in white, with curiously folded handkerchiefs on their heads. There is now only one other place in England, at Matlock, in Derbyshire, where this curious custom survives.

FUNERAL GARLAND, ABBOT'S ANN.

These villages, together with Amport, Thruxton, Monxton, and East Cholderton, lie in the triangular district between the branching of the two great routes of the road to Exeter. Just out of Andover, on the rising road, stands the old toll-house that commanded either route, with the mileage to various towns still displayed prominently on its walls. The right-hand road leads to the Weyhill and Amesbury branch of the Exeter Road, while the left-hand fork is the main road to Salisbury. Passing this toll-house, the old road runs through an inhospitable succession of uplands which are for the most part a weariness alike to mind and body, whether you walk, or cycle, or drive a horse, or urge forth your wild career on a motor-car. Going westwards, the gradient is chiefly a rising one for a long distance after leaving Andover behind, and it is not until 'the Wallops' are reached, at Little (or Middle) Wallop, lying in a hollow where a little stream trickles across the road, that any relief is experienced.

It must be Little Wallop to which Mr. Thomas Hardy refers in the *Mayor of Casterbridge*, where the ruined and broken-hearted Henchard, after taking up his early occupation of hay-trusser, becomes employed at a 'pastoral farm near the old western highway. . . . He had chosen the neighbourhood of this artery from a sense that, situated here, though at a distance of fifty miles, he was virtually nearer to her whose welfare was so dear than he would be at a roadless spot only half as remote.'

The Wallops are interesting places, despite their silly name. There are Over, and Nether, and Middle, or, as they are otherwise styled, Upper, Lower, and Little Wallop. According to one school of antiquaries (who must by no means be suspected of joking), the Wallop district is to be identified with the 'Gualoppum' described by an old chronicler, a district, appropriately enough, the scene of a great battle in which Vortigern was defeated by the Saxons. There are, of course, local derivations of the meaning of this place-name, together with a belief that to Sir John Wallop, an ancestor of the Earl of Portsmouth, who 'walloped the French' in one or other of our many mediaeval battles with that nation, we owe that very active, not to say slangy verb, 'to wallop.' But, unhappily for unscientific theories, there is a little stream, called the Wallop, flowing through these villages, to which they owe their generic name: the name of the stream itself deriving from the Anglo-

Saxon 'Weallan,' to boil or bubble; the root of our English word 'well.'

Of these villages, Little Wallop alone is on the road, and is merely an offshoot of the others, called into existence by the traffic which followed this course in the old coaching days. Since railways have left the roads lonely it has simply slumbered, 'far from the madding crowd's ignoble strife,' and its inhabitants are presumably happy in their retirement; although, when days are short and nights are long, and the stormy winds do blow, it is quite conceivable that there are more cheerful and warmer situations.

Three miles from here the road leaves Hampshire and enters Wilts, and two miles onwards from that point, after passing 'Lobcombe Corner,' the junction of the Stockbridge road, is seen that famous old coaching inn, the 'Pheasant,' known much better under its other name, 'Winterslow Hut.'

XXIII

There are few more desolate and cheerless places in England than the spot where this old coaching inn stands beside the open road, with the unenclosed downs stretching away to the far horizon, fold after fold. Somewhere amid these hills and hollows, but quite hidden, is the village of West Winterslow, from which the 'Hut' obtains its name. The place, save for the periodical passing of the coaches, was as solitary in old times as it is now, and its quiet as profound. The very name is chilling, and as excellently descriptive as it is possible for a name to be.

When, coming within sight of its isolated roof-tree from the summit of the hills on either side, the coach-guards used to blow fanfares on their bugles as a reminder for the ostler to have his fresh teams ready, the inn and its surrounding stables woke into life, and when they were gone their several ways, it dozed again. Save that it doubtless looked more prosperous then, the present appearance of 'Winterslow Hut' is identical with its aspect of sixty years ago. The same horse-pond by the roadside, the same trees, only older and more decrepit, the same pre-historic dykes and tumuli on the unchanging downs; it must have been capable of absorbing the fun and jollity of a fair, and still presenting its characteristically dour and dreary aspect; but now that, sitting in the bay window of the parlour that commands the road in either direction, you may watch the highway by the half-hour and see no traveller, the emptiness is appalling.

To this solitary outpost of civilisation came William Hazlitt, critic and essayist, during several years, for quietude. For four years, from 1808 to 1812, he and his wife lived in a cottage at West Winterslow, on the small income derived from her other cottage property there, supplemented by the sums the wayward Hazlitt earned fitfully by the practice of literature. Then they removed to London, where they disagreed, Hazlitt retiring to the 'Hut' in 1819, and leaving his wife in town. Nervous and irritable, he wanted quiet, nor can it be doubted that in this spot he found what he sought. He was cursed, according to the widely different beliefs of his friends, with 'an ingrained selfishness,' or 'a morbid self-consciousness,' and on the downs he would walk, for the pleasure of having the neighbourhood all to himself, from forty to fifty miles a day. He wrote his *Winterslow* essays here, and his *Napoleon*, for whom he had an almost insane reverence. The 'diabolical scowl' of Hazlitt when Napoleon or any other of his pet susceptibilities were abused must have been worth seeing.

'Now,' says a literary hero-hunter, who has visited 'Winterslow Hut,' as a place of pilgrimage,—'now it is a desolate place, fallen into decay, and tenanted by a labouring man and his family, cultivating a small farm of some thirty acres, and barely able to make a living out of it. In winter two or three weeks will sometimes elapse without even a beggar or tramp or cart passing the door. On the ground floor, looking out upon a horse-pond, flanked by two old lime-trees, is a little parlour, which was the one probably used by Hazlitt as his sitting-room. At the other end of the house is a large empty room, formerly devoted to cock-fighting matches and singlestick combats. It was with a strange and eerie feeling that I contemplated this little parlour, and pictured to myself the many solitary evenings during which Hazlitt sat in it enjoying copious libations of his favourite tea (for during the last fifteen years of his life he never tasted alcoholic drinks of any kind) perhaps reading *Tom Jones* for the tenth time, or enjoying

'WINTERSLOW HUT.

one of Congreve's comedies, or Rousseau's *Confessions*, or writing, in his large flowing hand, a dozen pages of the essay on *Persons one would Wish to have Seen*, or *On Living to One's Self*. One cannot imagine any retreat more consonant with the feelings of this lonely thinker, during one of his periods of seclusion, than the out-of-the-world place in which I stood. In winter time it must have been desolate beyond description—on wild nights especially—"heaven's chancel-vault" blind with sleet—the fierce wind sweeping down from the bare wolds around, and beating furiously against the doors and windows of the unsheltered hostelry.'

It is not to be supposed that Hazlitt was insensible to the dreariness of the spot. 'Here, *even* here,' he says, as though the dolour of the place had come home to him, 'with a few old authors I can manage to get through the summer or winter months without ever knowing what it is to feel *ennui*. They sit with me at breakfast; they walk out with me before dinner. After a long walk through unfrequented tracts, after starting the hare from the fern, or hearing the wing of the raven rustling above my head, or being greeted by the woodman's "stern good-night," as he strikes into his narrow homeward path, I can "take mine ease at mine inn," beside the blazing hearth, and shake hands with Signor Orlando Friscobaldo, as the oldest acquaintance I have.'

His *Farewell to Essay Writing* was written here 20th February 1828. He had long given up the intemperance of former years, and cultivated literature on copious tea-drinking. 'As I quaff my libations of tea in a morning,' he says, 'I love to watch the clouds sailing from the west, and fancy that "the spring comes slowly up this way." In this hope, while "fields are dank, and ways are mire," I follow the same direction to a neighbouring wood, where, having gained the dry, level greensward, I can see my way for a mile before me, closed in on each side by copse-wood, and ending in a point of light more or less brilliant, as the day is bright or cloudy.' And so this harbinger of our own literary neurotics continues, dropping into a morbid introspective strain, pulling up his soul, like a plant, by the roots, to see how it is growing, and babbling to the world, between the jewel-work of his literature, of his follies and his unrest. Strange, that this wiry pedestrian, this apostle of fresh air, should be of the same dough of which the degenerates of our time are compounded.

XXIV

It was here, however, that one of the most thrilling episodes of the road was enacted in the old days. The Mail from Exeter to London had left Salisbury on the night of 20th October 1816, and proceeded in the usual way for several miles, when what was thought to be a large calf was seen trotting beside the horses in the darkness. The team soon became extremely nervous and fidgety, and as the inn was approached they could scarcely be kept under control.

At the moment when the coachman pulled up to deliver his bags, one of the leading horses was suddenly seized by the supposed calf. The horses kicked and plunged violently, and it was with difficulty the driver could prevent the coach from being overturned. The guard drew his blunderbuss and was about to shoot the mysterious assailant when several men, accompanied by a large mastiff, appeared in sight. The foremost, seeing that the guard was about to fire, pointed a pistol at his head, swearing that he would be shot if the beast was killed.

Every one then perceived that this ferocious 'calf' was nothing less than a lioness. The dog was set on to attack her, and she thereupon left the horse and turned on him. He turned and ran, but the lioness caught him and tore him to pieces, carrying the remains in her mouth under a granary. The spot was then barricaded to prevent her escape, and a noose being thrown over her neck, she was secured and marched off to captivity again.

It is said that the horse when attacked fought with great spirit, and would probably have beaten off his assailant with his fore-feet had he been at liberty; but in his frantic plunges he became entangled in the harness. The lioness, it seems, attacked him in front, springing at his throat and fastening the claws of her fore-feet on either side of the neck, while her hind-feet tore at his chest. The horse, although fearfully mangled, survived. The showmen of the time were evidently quite as enterprising as those of these latter days, for the menagerie proprietor purchased the horse and exhibited him the next day at Salisbury Fair, with excellent results in the shape of increased gate-money.

The passengers on this extraordinary occasion were absolutely terror-stricken. Bounding off the coach, they made a wild rush for the inn, and, reaching the door, slammed it to and bolted it, to the exclusion of one poor fellow who, not active enough, found himself shut out in the road. The lioness, pursuing the dog, actually brushed against him. When she was secured, the poltroons inside the house opened the door and let the half-fainting traveller in. They gave him refreshments, and he recovered sufficiently to be able to write an account of the event for the local papers; but in a few days he became a raving maniac, and was sent to an asylum at Laverstock. For over twenty-seven years he lived there, incurable, and died in 1843.

The leader attacked by the lioness was a famous horse, even before that affair. There were many such in the coaching age. Animals unmanageable on the racecourse were frequently sold to coach-proprietors, and soon learnt discipline on the roads. 'Pomegranate' was his name. A 'thief' on the course, and a bad-tempered brute in the stable, he had worked on the Exeter Mail for some time before this dramatic episode in his career found him, for a time, a home in a menagerie.

The fame of the affair was great and lasting. That coaching specialist, James Pollard, drew, and R. Havell engraved, a plate showing the dramatic scene, which was dedicated to Thomas Hasker,

Superintendent of His Majesty's Mails. In it you see Joseph Pike, the guard, rising to shoot the very heraldic-looking lioness, and the passengers encouraging him in the background, from the safe retreat of the first-floor windows. It will be observed that this is apparently the lioness's first spring, and yet those passengers are already upstairs: at once a striking testimony to their agility and a warranty of the exquisite truth of the saying that fear lends wings to the feet.

XXV

Salisbury spire and the distant city come with the welcome surprise of a Promised Land after these bleak downs. Even three miles away the unenclosed wilds are done, and we drop continuously from Three Mile Hill, down, down, down to the lowlands on a smooth and uninterrupted road, to where the trees and the houses can be distinguished, nestling around and below the graceful cathedral, a long way yet ahead. It is coming thus with that needle-pointed spire, so long and so prominently in view, that the story of its having been built to its extraordinary height of 404 feet for the purpose of guiding the strayed footsteps of travellers across the solitudes of Salisbury Plain may readily be believed.

Salisbury wears a bland and cheerful appearance, and has an air of modernity that quite belies its age. Few places in England have so well-ascertained an origin. We can fix the very year, six hundred and eighty years ago, when it began to be, and yet, although there is the cathedral to prove its age, with the Poultry Cross, and very many ancient houses happily still standing, it has a general air of anything but mediaevalism. This curious feeling that strikes every visitor is really owing to the generous and well-ordered plan on which the city was originally laid out; broad streets being planned in geometrical precision, and the blocks of houses built in regular squares.

That phenomenally simple-minded person, Tom Pinch, thought Salisbury 'a very desperate sort of place; an exceedingly wild and dissipated city'—a view of it which is not shared by any one else. I wish I could tell you to which inn it was that he resorted to have dinner, and to await the arrival of Martin. A coaching inn, of course, for Martin came by coach from London. But whether it was the 'White Hart,' or the 'Three Swans' (which, alas! is no longer an inn), or the 'King's Arms,' or the 'George,' is more than I or any one else can determine.

Salisbury is by no means desperate or dissipated, even though it be market-day, and although itinerant cutlery vendors may still sell seven-bladed knives, with never a cut among them, to the unwary. It is true that Mr. Thomas Hardy has given us, in *On the Western Circuit*, a picture of blazing orgies at Melchester Fair, with steam-trumpeting merry-go-rounds, glamour and glitter, glancing young women no better than they ought to be, and an amorous young barrister much worse than he should have been; and it is true that by 'Melchester' this fair city of Salisbury is meant; but you can conjure up no very accurate picture of this ancient place from those pages. The real Salisbury is extremely urbane and polished, decorous and well-ordered. It is graceful and sunny, and has, in fact, all the sweetness of mediaevalism without its sternness, and affords a thorough contrast with Winchester, which frowns upon you where Salisbury smiles. One need not waver from one's allegiance to Winchester to admit so much.

Salisbury is still known in official documents as 'New Sarum.' It is, nevertheless, of a quite respectable antiquity, its newness dating from that day, 28th April 1220, when Bishop Poore laid the foundation-stone of the still existing cathedral. There are romantic incidents in the exodus from Old Sarum on its windy height upon the downs, a mile and a half away, to these 'rich champaign fields and fertile valleys, abounding with the fruits of the earth, and watered by living streams,' in this 'sink of Salisbury Plain,' where the Bourne, the Wylye, the Avon, and the Nadder flow in innumerable runlets through the meads.

Old Sarum was old indeed. Its history strikes rootlets deep down into the Unknown. A natural hillock upon the wild downs, its defensible position rendered it a camp for the earliest aboriginal tribes, who, always at war with one another, lived for safety's sake in such bleak and inhospitable places when they would much rather be hunting and enjoying life generally in the sheltered wooded vales and fertile plains. These tribes heaped up the first artificial earthworks that ever strengthened this historic hill, and they were succeeded during the long march of those dim centuries by Romans, Saxons, and Danes. The Romans, with their unerring military instinct, saw the importance of the hill, and added to the simple defences they found there. They called the place *Sorbiodunum*, and made it a great strategic station. The Saxons strengthened the fortifications in their turn, and at the time of the Norman Conquest a city had grown up under the shelter of the citadel.

In its deserted state to-day, the site of Old Sarum vividly recalls the appearance presented by an extinct volcano, the conical hill rising from the downs with the suddenness of an upheaval, and the area enclosed within the concentric rings of banks and ditches forming a hollow space similar to a crater. The total area enclosed within these fortifications is about 28 acres. Within this space was comprised that ancient city, and in its very centre, overlooking everything else, and encompassed by a circular fosse and bank, 100 feet in height, stood the citadel. The site of this castle is now overgrown with dense thickets of shrubs and brambles; the fragments of its flint and rubble walls, 12 feet thick, and some remaining portions of its gateways affording evidence of its old-time strength.

Within this city, enclosed for centuries by the ring-fence of these fortifications, stood the cathedral, in a position just below the Castle ward. Its exact site and size (although not a fragment of it is standing) were discovered in the summer of 1834. That portion of the vanished city had been laid down as pasture, and the drought of that year revealed the plan of the cathedral, in a distinct brown outline upon the grass. This building, completed in 1092 by Bishop Osmund, furnished the stone in later years for the spire of Salisbury Cathedral and for the walls of the Close, in which, by St. Anne's Gate, many sculptured fragments of these relics from Old Sarum may yet be seen.

A variety of circumstances brought about the removal of the cathedral from Old Sarum. Water was lacking on that height, and winds raged so furiously around it that the monks could not hear the priests say Mass; and, worse than all, during the Papal Interdict, the King, in revenge for many ecclesiastical annoyances, transferred the custody of the Castle of Old Sarum from the bishops to his own creatures, who locked the monks out of their monastery and church on one occasion when they had gone on some religious procession. When the monks returned, they found entrance denied them, and were forced to remain in the open air during the whole of a frosty winter night. There was no end to the hardships which those Men of Wrath brought upon the Church. No wonder that Peter of Blois cried out, 'What has the House of the Lord to do with castles? It is the Ark of the Covenant in the Temple of Baalim. Let us in God's name descend into the plain.'

The removal decided upon, it remained to choose a site. Tradition tells us that the Virgin Mary appeared to Bishop Poore in a vision, and told him to build the church on a spot called Merryfield; and has it that the site was chosen by the fall of an arrow shot from the ramparts of Old Sarum. If that was the case, there must have been something miraculous in that shot, for the place where Salisbury Cathedral is built is a mile and a half away from those ramparts. But perhaps the bishop or the legends used the long bow in a very special sense.

The cathedral was completed in sixty years, receiving its final consecration in 1260; but the great spire was not finished until a hundred years later. The city was an affair of rapid growth, receiving a charter of incorporation seven years after being founded. Seventeen years later, Bishop Bingham dealt a final blow at the now utterly ruined city of Old Sarum by diverting the old Roman road to the West from its course through Old Sarum, Bemerton, and Wilton, and making a highway running directly to New Sarum, and crossing the Avon by the new bridge which he had built at Harnham. Old Sarum could by this time make little or no resistance, for it was deserted, save for a few who could not bring themselves to leave the home of their forefathers. Wilton, however, which was a thriving town, bitterly resented this diversion of the roads, and petitioned against it, but without avail. From that date Wilton's decline set in, and the rise of New Sarum progressed at an even greater speed. A clothing trade sprang up and prospered, and many Royal visits gave the citizens an air of importance. They waxed rich and arrogant, and were eternally

quarrelling with the bishops, one of whom they murdered in the turbulent times that prevailed during Jack Cade's rebellion. Bishop Ayscough was that unfortunate prelate. He had cautiously retired to Edington, but a furious body of Salisbury malcontents marched out across the Plain, and dragging him from the altar of the church, where he was saying Mass, took him to an adjacent hill-top, and slew him with the utmost barbarity. It was for the benefit of these unruly citizens that one of Jack Cade's quarters was consigned from London to Salisbury and elevated there on a pole, as a preliminary warning. Full punishment followed a little later.

XXVI

It is really too great a task to follow the history of Salisbury through the centuries to the present time; nor, indeed, since the city and the cathedral are from our present point of view but incidents along the Exeter Road, would it be desirable to dwell very long on their story, which, as may have been judged from what has already been said, is an exceedingly turbulent one. The fearful martyrdoms carried out in Fisherton Fields by the bloody hell-hounds of the Marian Persecution still stain the records of the Church; nor, although the very reading of them turn brain and body sick, and make even the architectural enthusiast almost turn away in disgust from that lovely cathedral, may God grant that they ever be forgotten, as in the England of to-day they would almost seem to be. Hellish ferocity, damnable frauds, how they smirch those sculptured stones and cry insistently for remembrance!

Nicholas Shaxton, Bishop in the time of Henry the Eighth, was alive to it all, and cleared away the false relics; the 'stinking boots, mucky combs, ragged rochetts, rotten girdles, pyled purses, great bullocks' horns, locks of hair, filthy rags, and gobbets of wood,' which he found here; but, with less courage than others, he recanted in Mary's reign. Sherfield, Recorder of Salisbury, was another reformer, but he lived in less dangerous times for such men. It was in 1629 that he smashed the stained-glass window, representing the Creation, in St. Edmund's Church. In other times he would assuredly have been burnt for this act; as it was, he was summoned before the Star Chamber. He pleaded that the window did not contain a true history of the Creation, and objected that God was represented as 'a little old man in a long blue coat,' which he held was 'an indignity offered to Almighty God.' He was committed to the Fleet Prison for this, fined £500, and required to apologise to the Bishop of Salisbury. Fortunate Mr. Sherfield!

This fair city has been almost as much of a Golgotha as the settlements of savage African kinglets are wont to be. Shakespeare has made mention of the execution of the Duke of Buckingham here in 1484 by Richard the Third, but many an one has suffered and left no such trace. That such executions were generally unjust and almost always too severe is their sufficient condemnation; but the hanging of Charles, Lord Stourton, in 1556, is an exception. The affair for which he was put to death was the murder of the two Hartgills, father and son, at Kilmington, Somerset, and it affords an unusually instructive glimpse into the manners of the period. It seems that William Hartgill had long been steward to the previous Lord Stourton, the father of Charles. Like most stewards, he had profited by his stewardship, over and above his salary, to a considerable extent. There was no friendship wasted between him and the new lord, but the quarrels which had taken place between William Hartgill and his son on the one side, and Charles, Lord Stourton, and his servants on the other, finally came to a head when my lord demanded a written undertaking from his mother that she would never marry again, and that Hartgill should be bond for the undertaking being kept. The widowed Lady Stourton was residing at the Hartgills' house when this demand was made. She refused to have anything to do with such a paper, and Hartgill bluntly declined as well. Lord Stourton would then appear to have determined on revenge for this defeat, and eventually, after the Hartgills had been on several occasions waylaid, threatened, and attacked by his servants, he conceived the devilish plan of a pretended reconciliation over this and other disputes in the village churchyard of Kilmington, the occasion to be used as a means of taking them off their guard, and finally disposing of them. The two victims were suspicious of this apparent friendliness; but, unhappily for them, eventually agreed to meet in that God's Acre, on 12th January 1556, there to settle all accounts and differences. They met, and, at a previously arranged signal, Lord Stourton's servants rushed upon the Hartgills and stabbed and battered them to death in a revoltingly cruel manner, while their master looked on with approval. The details of this cold-blooded atrocity are fully set forth in the trials of that period, for the satisfaction of any one greedy of horrors.

This was in the reign of Queen Mary, when Protestants were burned at the stake with the approval of Roman Catholics; but not even in those brutal times could this affair be hushed up. Lord Stourton was arrested, brought to trial in London, and, together with four of his servants, found guilty of murder, and sentenced to death. Justice was commendably swift. The two Hartgills had been done to death on the 12th of January, and on the second day of March in the same year my lord set out under escort from the Tower of London for Salisbury, the place of execution. The melancholy cavalcade came down the Exeter Road, the chief figure in it set astride a horse, with legs and arms pinioned. The first night they lay at Hounslow, the second at Staines, the third at Basingstoke, and thence to Salisbury, where, in the Market Place, on the morning of the 6th of March, they hanged him with a silken cord. His servants were turned off at the end of quite common hempen ropes, which doubtless did their business quite as neatly. The body of this prime malefactor, the organiser of the crime, was buried with much ceremony in the cathedral, but those of the lesser criminals were treated (we may suppose) with less reverence, because you may search the building in vain for tomb or epitaph to their memory. But—quaintest touch of all—the silken rope by which Lord Stourton swung was suspended here, over his tomb, where it remained for many a long year afterwards.

The next outstanding landmark in the way of executions is the hanging of a prisoner who had just been awarded a sentence when he threw a brickbat at the Chief Justice. His lordship was considerably damaged and for this assault pronounced sentence of death upon him. The execution took place at once, outside the Council House, the unfortunate man's right hand being first struck off.

The Civil War did not result in anything very tragical for Salisbury, the operations in and around the city being quite unimportant. The 'Catherine Wheel Inn,' however, was the scene of much alarm among the superstitious, when, according to a gruesome story, the Cavaliers assembled there, having toasted the King and the Royal family, proceeded to drink the health of the Devil, and the Devil appeared, the room becoming filled with 'noisome fumes of sulphur, and a hideous monster, which was the Devil, no doubt,' entering, and grabbing the giver of the toast, flying away with him out of the window.

Salisbury was the scene of Penruddocke's rising for the King in 1655. He was a county gentleman, of Compton Chamberlayne, and with some others and a band of a hundred and fifty horsemen, rode into the city at four o'clock in the morning of 14th March. They seized the Judges of Assize in their beds, opened the doors of the prison, and imprisoned the judges in the place of the released convicts. Then, finding the citizens too timid to join them in their revolt against Cromwell, they sped across country, into Devon, where they were captured.

Charles the Second was welcomed by Salisbury's citizens, just as they welcomed every one else; practising with much success St. Paul's admirable precept, to be 'all things to all men.' When James the Second came here, on his way to meet, and fight, the Prince of Orange, he was escorted, with every show of deference and respect, to his lodgings at the Bishop's Palace by the Mayor, and when he had slunk away, and the Prince came, less than four weeks later, and was lodged in the same house, the same Mayor did precisely the same thing.

From the beginning of the seventeenth century onward the citizens began to dearly love kings and great personages, or, if they did not love them, effectually pretended to do so. When plague ravaged the city of London, no one coming from that direction was allowed to enter Salisbury, and even Salisbury's own citizens returning home from that infected centre were obliged to remain outside for three months, while goods were not permitted to be brought nearer than Three Mile Hill. But Charles the Second and his Court, flying from London from the disease, were welcomed all the same!

XXVII

Coach passengers entering Salisbury even so late as 1835 were sometimes witnesses of shocking scenes that, however picturesque they might have rendered mediæval times, were brutalising and degrading in a civilised era. Almost every year of the nineteenth century up to that date was fruitful in executions. In 1801 there were ten: seven for the crime of sheep-stealing, one for horse-stealing, one for stealing a calf, and one for highway robbery. The practice of hanging criminals on the scenes of their crimes afforded spectacles of the most extraordinary character, as instanced in the procession that accompanied two murderers, George Carpenter and George Ruddock, from Fisherton Gaol, on the north-west of the city, to the place of their execution on Warminster Down, 15th March 1813. Such parades were senseless, since no one ever dreamed of a rescue being attempted; but, all the same, the condemned men, placed in a cart and accompanied by a clergyman preaching of Kingdom Come, preceded by the hangman and followed by eight men carrying two coffins, were escorted all the way by a troop of Wiltshire Yeomanry, followed by some two hundred constables and local gentlemen, all walking and carrying white staves; with bailiffs, sheriffs, under-sheriffs, magistrates, a hundred mounted squires, a posse of 'javelin men,' more clergymen, the gaoler and his assistants, more javelin men and sheriff's officers, more yeomanry, and, at last, bringing up the rear, a howling mob, numbering many thousands. As for the central objects in this show, 'they died penitent,' we are told; and indeed they could do nothing less, seeing to what trouble they had thus put a goodly proportion of the county.

Executions for all manner of crimes were so many that it would be idle to detail them; but some stand out prominently by reason of their circumstances. For example, the hanging of Robert Turner Watkins in 1819, for a murder near Purton, presents a lurid scene. His wife had died of a broken heart shortly after his arrest, and his mother was among the spectators of his end. The same kind of procession accompanied him across Salisbury Plain to the place of execution, and a similar mob made the occasion a holiday. Mother and son were able to bid one another farewell, owing to an unexpected halt on the road; and when they made a halt for the refreshments which the long journey demanded, the condemned man's children were brought to him. 'Mammy is dead,' said one. 'Ah!' replied the man, 'and so will your daddy be, shortly.' At the fatal spot he prayed with the chaplain, and was allowed to read to the people a psalm which he had chosen. It was Psalm 108, which, on reference, will not prove to be particularly appropriate to the occasion. Then he blessed the fifteen thousand or so present, felt the rope, and remarked that it could only kill the body, and was turned off, amid the sudden and unexpected breaking of one of the most terrific thunderstorms ever experienced on the Plain.

They hanged a gipsy, one Joshua Shemp, in 1801,

for stealing a horse, and afterwards discovered that he was innocent, according to a monument still to be seen in Odstock churchyard. In 1802 John Everett suffered death for uttering forged bank-notes, followed in 1820 by William Lee, who died for the same offence. So late as 1835, two men were hanged for arson; but public opinion had already been aroused against such severity, judges and juries taking every advantage offered by faults in the drawing up of indictments to acquit all those criminals not guilty of murder whose crimes were then met by capital punishment. The statutes left no choice but death for the convicted incendiary, the horse- or sheep-stealer, and many another; and so many a guilty person was acquitted by judges and juries horrified by the thought of incurring blood-guiltiness by sending such men to the scaffold. The law allowed loopholes for escape, and so when the *straw*-rick, to which a prisoner was charged with setting fire, was proved to have been *hay*, he was found 'Not guilty.' Blackstone called this action taken by juries 'pious perjury,' and so it certainly was when, to avoid shedding blood, they used to find £5 and £10 notes which prisoners sometimes were charged with stealing, to be articles to the value of twelvepence or a few shillings, according as the case required.

The last lawless scenes around Salisbury were enacted at the close of 1830, when the so-called 'Machinery Riots,' which had spread all over the country, culminated here in fights between the Wiltshire Yeomanry and the discontented agricultural labourers, who, fearing that steam machinery, then beginning to be adopted, was about to take away their livelihood, scoured the country in bands, wrecking and burning farmsteads and barns. The 'Battle of Bishop Down,' on the Exeter Road between 'Winterslow Hut' and Salisbury, was fought on

ST. ANNE'S GATE, SALISBURY

23rd November, and was caused by the collision of a large body of rioters who were marching to the city with the avowed object of pillaging it, and a mixed force of yeomanry and special constables. All the coaches, together with every other kind of traffic, were brought to a standstill. Stone-throwing on the part of the rioters, and bludgeoning by the special constables were succeeded by charges of the yeomanry, and the contest resulted in the capture of twenty-two rioters, who were locked up in Fisherton Gaol. The next day a number of rioters were surprised in the 'Green Dragon Inn,' Alderbury, and marched off to prison; and the day after, twenty-five were taken in a fight near Tisbury, after one of their number had been killed. There were no fewer than three hundred and thirty prisoners awaiting trial when the Special Commissioners arrived for that purpose on 27th December. Many of the prisoners were transported, and others had short terms of imprisonment; but a leader, called 'Commander' Coote, who was captured by two constables at the Compasses, Rockbourn, was hanged at Winchester.

XXVIII

And now for some little-known literary landmarks. Salisbury, of course, is the scene of some passages in *Martin Chuzzlewit;* but it is outside the city that we must go, on the road to Southampton, to find the residence of that eminent architect, Mr. Pecksniff; or the 'Blue Dragon,' where Tom Pinch's friend, Mrs. Lupin, was landlady. St. Mary's Grange, four miles from Salisbury, is the real name of Mr. Pecksniff's home, but the house is only vaguely indicated in the novel. It is different with the 'Blue Dragon,' which is an undoubted portrait of the 'Green Dragon Inn,' at Alderbury, despite the fact that the sign-board has since disappeared. 'A faded, and an ancient dragon he was; and many a wintry storm of rain, snow, sleet, and hail had changed his colour from a gaudy blue to a faint, lack-lustre shade of grey. But there he hung; rearing in a state of monstrous imbecility on his hind legs; waxing, with every month that passed, so much more dim and shapeless, that as you gazed on him at one side of the sign-board, it seemed as if he must be gradually melting through it, and coming out upon the other.'

The 'Green Dragon' is a quaint gabled village inn, standing back from the road. It is even more ancient than any one, judging only from its exterior, would suppose, for a fine fifteenth-century mantel-piece, adorned with carved crockets and heraldic roses, yet remains in the parlour, a relic of bygone importance.

As for Mrs. Lupin, the landlady, it is supposed that Dickens drew the character from a real person. If so, how one would like to have known that cheery woman. Do you remember how Tom Pinch left Salisbury to seek his fortune in London? and how Mrs. Lupin met the coach on the London road with his box in the trap, and a great basket of provisions, with a bottle of sherry sticking out of it? and how the open-handed fellow shared the cold roast fowl, the packet of ham in slices, the crusty loaf, and the other half-dozen items—not forgetting the contents of the bottle—with the coachman and guard as they drove along the old road to London through the night?

'Yoho, past hedges, gates, and trees; past cottages and barns, and people going home from work. Yoho, past donkey-chaises, drawn aside into the ditch, and empty carts with rampant horses, whipped up at a bound upon the little watercourse, and held by struggling carters close to the five-barred gate, until the coach had passed the narrow turning in the road. Yoho, by churches dropped down by themselves in quiet nooks, with rustic burial-grounds about them, where graves are green, and daisies sleep—for it is evening—on the bosoms of the dead. Yoho, past streams in which the cattle cool their feet, and where the rushes grow; past paddock-fences, farms and rick-yards; past last year's stacks, cut slice by slice away, and showing in the waning light like ruined gables, old and brown. Yoho, down the pebbly dip, and through the merry water-splash, and up at a canter to the level road again. Yoho! Yoho!'

Quite so. And an excellent picture of the coaching age, although 'Yoho!' smacks too much of the sea for a coach. In his haste he wrote that word when he surely meant 'Tallyho!' Nor is this a correct portrait of the Exeter Road by any manner of means. Dickens, usually so precise in topographical details, has generalised here. A true and stirring picture of country roads in general, there are farms, and villages, and churches all too many for this highway. It should have been 'Yoho! across the bleak and barren down. Yoho! by the blasted oak on the lonely common,' and so forth, so far as Andover, at any rate. And what was that water-splash doing on a main road in the flower of the coaching age, when all the runnels and streams across the mail routes were duly bridged? But it is not very odd that Dickens should have been so inexact here, for he began *Martin Chuzzlewit* in 1843, and it was not until long after the book was published, in 1848, that he really explored the Exeter Road. Forster tells us that Dickens, in company with himself, Leech, and Lemon, stayed at Salisbury in the March of that year, and 'passed a March day in riding over every part of the Plain; visiting Stonehenge, and exploring Hazlitt's "Hut" at Winterslow.'

It must be obvious how exquisitely fitted, both by reason of its situation and circumstances, 'Winterslow Hut' is for the novelist's use, and that, had he explored it before, that wild spot would have found a place in the pages of *Martin Chuzzlewit*, together with detailed references to some of Salisbury's old coaching inns, of which there were many, this being a meeting-place of several roads, besides being on the great highway to the West.

So far back as 1786 there were three coaches passing through Salisbury on their way from London to Exeter, daily. Firstly, the 'Post Coach' every morning at eight o'clock, with the up coach to London every afternoon at four o'clock, Saturdays excepted. Secondly, a mail coach, specially advertised as carrying a guard all the way, every morning at ten o'clock, Sundays excepted, and the up mail every night at ten o'clock, Saturdays excepted. Thirdly, a 'Diligence,' which passed through every night about eight o'clock, the up coach at twelve, midnight. All these coaches stopped, and were horsed, at the 'White Hart.' In 1797 there were five coaches to and from London, daily, and three on alternate days; and three waggons, two every day, the other on Tuesdays, Thursdays, and Saturdays.

In those times, when highwaymen were numerous and daring and travellers appropriately anxious, stage-coach proprietors in Salisbury advertised the fact of their conveyances being provided with an armed guard, and that any one making an attempt at robbery would be handed over to justice. But, notwithstanding such bold announcements, all the friends and relatives of citizens daring the journey to London used to assemble on the London road and tearfully watch the coaches as they toiled up Bishop Down and over the crest of Three Mile Hill, into the Unknown. The spot is still called 'Weeping Cross.'

Of the old Salisbury coaching inns, a goodly number have been either pulled down or converted to other purposes. The 'King's Head,' the 'Maidenhead,' the 'Sun,' the 'Vine,' the 'Three Tuns,' and others have entirely disappeared; and the 'Spread Eagle,' the 'Lamb,' 'Three Cups,' 'Antelope,' and the 'George'—where Pepys stayed and was overcharged—have become shops or private residences; while the beautiful old 'Three Swans' was converted into a Temperance Hotel five years ago.

There is a passage in Sir William Knighton's Diary under date of 1832, which, although written without any special emphasis, is highly picturesque and informative on the subject of travelling at that time. It gives in one phrase a glimpse of the waiting-room which was a feature of all-coaching inns, and in another shows that it was possible to bargain for fares. Only in this instance the bargain was not struck.

He had come at half-past one in the morning into Salisbury by a cross-country coach, and waiting for the arrival of the mail to Exeter, 'sat quietly by the fire in the common dirty room appropriated to coach passengers.'

For twenty minutes, he says, he had for companion a man who had just disengaged himself from an irritable rencontre with the coachman of the mail. He had waited from two o'clock in the afternoon to go on to Bristol, but when the time arrived he quarrelled with the coachman about whether he should pay nine shillings or twelve, the passenger insisting upon nine, the whip three shillings more; upon which the traveller decided not to go, returned to the coach-room, and ordered his bed. Sir William asked him if it really was worth while to lose the time and to pay for a bed at the inn over this unsuccessful negotiation, and to this the man replied that it was not. 'In fact,' said he, 'we have both been taken in. The coachman thought I would pay, and I thought he would take my offer.'

XXIX

It is a nine-miles journey, due north from Salisbury to Stonehenge, but although it would, under

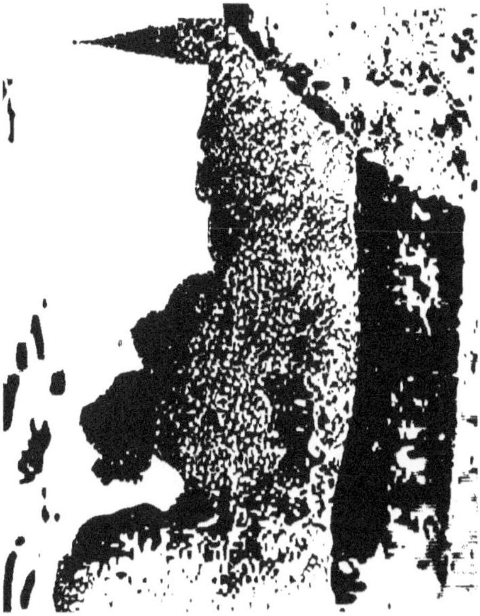

other circumstances, be unduly extending the scope of this work to travel so far from the highway, we need have no compunction in making this trip, for it brings us to one of the most interesting places on the Amesbury and Ilminster route to Exeter—to Stonehenge, in fact, and passes by the wonderful terraced hill of Old Sarum. You can see Old Sarum looming ahead immediately after passing the outlying houses of Salisbury, and if you come upon it when a storm is impending, as in Constable's picture, the impression of size and strength created is one not soon to be forgotten. As to coming upon it in the dark, as Pepys did, the sight is awe-inspiring.

Time and place conspired to frighten him. 'So over the Plain,' he says, 'by the sight of the steeple, to Salisbury by night; but before I came to the town, I saw a great fortification, and there alighted, and to it, and in it; and find it prodigious, so as to fright me to be in it all alone at that time of night, it being dark. I understand since it to be that that is called Old Sarum.'

To climb the steep grassy ramparts, one after the other, and to descend into and climb out of the successive yawning ditches is a tiring exercise, but perhaps in no other way is it possible to gain anything like a proper idea of the strength of the place. Nor is there any more sure way of arriving at the relative scale of it than by observing the stray cyclist standing on the topmost ramparts and gazing toward the distant spire of Salisbury.

There are other things than ancient history that make Old Sarum memorable. It was the head and front of the electoral scandals that brought about the great Reform Act of 1832. Although it contained neither a single house nor an inhabitant, Old Sarum survived as a Parliamentary borough until that date, and regularly returned two members. Lord John Russell, introducing the Reform Bill to the House of Commons, remarked that Old Sarum was a green mound without a single habitation upon it, and like Gatton, also an uninhabited borough, returned two members, while great towns like Birmingham and Manchester were entirely without Parliamentary representation. The two members sent to Parliament were merely the nominees of the Lord of the Manor, elected by two dummy electors who, shortly after each dissolution of Parliament, were granted leases in the borough of Old Sarum—leases known as 'burgage tenures.' Their voting done, they quietly surrendered their leases, which were not granted again until a like occasion arose. The elections took place at the 'Parliament Tree,' which, until 1896 (when it was blown down in a snowstorm), stood in a meadow between the mound and the village of 'Stratford-under-the-Castle.' It was supposed to have marked the site of the Town Hall of the vanished town. Cobbett, riding horseback past the spot, anathematised this 'rotten borough' and the system that allowed such things. He calls it 'The Accursed Hill.' The only house standing near is the 'Old Castle Inn.'

Beyond it the road dips steeply to the downs, and so continues, with regular undulations, unsheltered from storms or frosts, or the fierce heat of the summer sun, to Amesbury.

OLD SARUM (AFTER CONSTABLE, R.A.).

Amesbury is a sheltered village, lying in a valley between these downs. It was on the alternative coach route taken by the 'Telegraph,' 'Celerity,' 'Defiance,' and 'Subscription' coaches, which, leaving Andover, came by Weyhill, Mullen's Pond, and 'Park House Inn.' This way came the 'Telegraph' coach on its journey to London, 27th December 1836, through the thick of that terrible snowstorm of which we find copious mention on every one of the classic roads. It began when they reached Wincanton, and from that place they struggled on up to the Plain, where it was a white world of scurrying snow-flakes, howling winds, and deep drifts. Down into Amesbury, and to the hospitable 'George' there, was but a momentary respite, for the determined coachman, although immediately snowed up in the open country beyond the village, sent for help and, assisted by a team of six fresh post-horses with a post-boy to every pair, charged up the hills in the direction of Andover, with that fortune which is said to favour the brave. That is to say, he and His Majesty's mails got through to London, where the story was duly chronicled in the papers of the period.

Here, or hereabouts, it was that the up Exeter 'Celerity' coach came into collision with the 'Defiance' at one o'clock in the morning of 25th July 1827, resulting in the death of a gentleman who was thrown off the roof of the 'Celerity' and instantly killed, and in serious injuries to others. Both coaches were overturned. The 'Celerity' coachman, according to the evidence at the subsequent trial, was to blame for reckless driving, and for endeavouring to take too much of the road; but the lawyers found a flaw in the indictment, which stated that he was driving three geldings and a mare, and as it could not be proved that this description was correct, the matter dropped.

XXX

And now to Stonehenge and Salisbury Plain, up the steep road from Amesbury taken by the coaches. Unless you can see Stonehenge in such an awful thunderstorm as Turner shows in his picture of it, or can come upon the place at dead of night either by moonlight, or in the blackness of a moonless midnight, you will fail to be impressed; unless you are a literary pilgrim and can be moved to sentiment, not by thoughts of the mythical human sacrifices offered up here by imaginary Druids, but by the last scenes in the tragedy of poor Tess. Then the place has an immediate human interest which otherwise it lacks in the immeasurably vast space of time dividing us from the period of its building and of the heaping up of the sepulchral barrows that make a wide circle round it on the Plain. Solitary, with nothing to give it scale, even the brakes that convey irreverent excursionists help to confer a dignity on the spot, when seen afar upon the ridge where this Mystery, sphinx-like, offers an insoluble riddle to archaeologists of all the ages.

No one, despite the affected archaisms and the

THE GREAT SNOWSTORM OF 1836; THE EXETER 'TELEGRAPH,' ASSISTED BY POST-HORSES, DRIVING THROUGH THE SNOW-DRIFTS AT AMESBURY (AFTER JAMES POLLARD).

sham archæology, has described Stonehenge so impressively as that 'wondrous boy' Chatterton :—

A wondrous pyle of rugged mountaynes standes,
Placed on eche other in a dreare arraie,
It ne could be the worke of human handes,
It ne was reared up by menne of claie.
Here did the Britons adoration paye
To the false god whom they did Tauran name,
Lightynge hys altarre with greate fyres in Maie,
Roasteyng theire victims round aboute the flame :
'Twas here that Hengyst dyd the Brytons slee,
As they were met in council for to bee.

Stonehenge was probably standing when the Romans came to Britain, and doubtless astonished them when they first saw it as much as any one else. Its surroundings were not very different then from now. A farmstead, with ugly blue-slated roof, which has appeared on the ridge of the down of late years, and possibly a road which did not exist in days of old : these alone have changed the aspect of the vast solitude in which the hoary monument stands. No hedges, no gates, never a sheep upon the meagre grass. As Ingoldsby says of Salisbury Plain, in general :—

Not a shrub, nor a tree, nor a bush can you see :
No hedges, no ditches, no gates, no stiles,
Much less a house or a cottage for miles.

This, saving that intrusive farmstead, still holds good here ; and although every one is inevitably disappointed with Stonehenge, as first seen at a distance, looking *so small* and insignificant in the vastness of the bare downs in which it is set, the place, and not the great stones merely, impresses by its sadness and utter detachment from the living world, its loves and hates and interests. The birds forget to sing in this loneliness, which is awful in winter and not less awful in the emptiness visible under the blue sky and blazing sun of summer. Just the situation in which Stonehenge is placed, you understand, not Stonehenge itself, gives these feelings. 'Do not we gaze with awe upon these massive stones?' asks the high-falutin guide-book compiler. No, indeed we don't. It is a pity, but it can't be done, and the average description of Stonehenge which sets forth the grandeur and stupendous size of these stones, is pumped-up fudge and flapdoodle of the damnablest kind, which takes in no one. It is not merely the Philistine who thinks thus, but even the would-be marvellers, and those of light and leading are disquieted by secret thoughts that, had we a mind to it, and if there was money in it, we could build a better and a bigger Stonehenge by a long way.

The earliest account of this mystic monument is found in the writings of Nennius, who lived in the ninth century. The first-comer is entitled to respect, and when Nennius tells us that Stonehenge was erected by the surviving Britons, in memory of four hundred and sixty British nobles, murdered here at a conference to which the Saxon chieftain, Hengist, had invited King Vortigern and his Court, we are bound to pay some attention to the statement, although to place implicit reliance upon it would be rash, considering the fact that Nennius wrote four hundred years after the event.

STONEHENGE (AFTER TURNER, R.A.)

But there are, and have been, many theories which profess to give the only true origin of these stone circles. An antiquary formerly living at Amesbury went to the beginnings of creation and held that they were erected by Adam. If so, it is to be hoped for Adam's sake that he finished the job in the summer, or that if it occupied him in winter time, he had clothed himself with something warmer than the traditional fig-leaf, in view of the rigours of these Wiltshire Downs. It would be interesting also to have Adam's opinion as to the comparative merits of Salisbury Plain and the Garden of Eden.

Then a tradition existed that Merlin, the sorcerer, arranged the circles. Those who do not think much of this view may take more kindly to the legend of our old friends the Druids, who, according to Dr. Stukeley and others, made this their chief temple: while, according to other views, the Britons before and after the Roman occupation, and the Romans themselves, were the builders. Then there are others who conceive this to have been the crowning-place of the Danish kings. The Saxons, indeed, appear to be the only people who have not been credited with the work; although, curiously enough, its very name is of Saxon derivation, and the earliest writers refer to it as 'Stanenges,' from Anglo-Saxon words meaning 'the hanging-stones.' That the Saxons discovered Stonehenge, and were puzzled by it as greatly as it must have excited the wonder of the Romans, hundreds of years before, seems obvious from this name they gave the lonely place. Ignorant as to its use, they either saw in the upright stones and the imposts they carried a resemblance to a gallows, or else, not being themselves expert builders, marvelled that the great imposts should remain suspended in the air.

Much of the legitimate wonderment in respect of Stonehenge lies in the mystery of how the forgotten builders could have quarried and shaped these stones, and could have cut the tenons and mortice-holes that held the tall columns, and the flat stones above them, together. Camden, the old chronicler, has a ready way out of this puzzling question. Beginning with a description of this 'huge and monstrous piece of work,' he goes on to say that 'some there are that think them to be no natural stones, hewn out of the rock, but artificially made out of pure sand, and, by some glue or unctuous matter, knit and incorporate together.'

Stonehenge is considered to have consisted, when perfect, of an outer circle of thirty tall stones, three and a half feet apart, and connected together by a line of imposts, in whose extremities mortice-holes were cut, fitting into corresponding tenons projecting from the upright stones. The height of this circular screen was sixteen feet. A second and inner circle consisted of smaller and rougher stones, some forty in number, and six feet in height. Within this circle, again, rose five tall groups of stone placed in an ellipse, each group consisting of two uprights, with an impost above. These stones were the largest of all, the tallest reaching to a height of twenty-five feet. They were named by Dr. Stukeley, impressively enough, the Great Trilithons. Each of these five groups would appear to have been accompanied on the inner side by a cluster of three small standing stones, while a black flat monolith, called the 'Altar Stone,' occupied the innermost position. A smaller trilithon seems to have once stood near its big brethren, but it and three of the great five are in ruins. Only six imposts of the outer circle are left in their place overhead, and but sixteen of its thirty upright stones are now standing. The smaller circles and groups are equally imperfect. Some of this ruin has befallen within the historical period; one of the Great Trilithons having been wrecked in 1620, in the absurd treasure-seeking expedition of the Duke of Buckingham, while another fell on the 3rd of January 1797, during a thaw.

These circles seem to have been surrounded by an earthen bank, with an avenue leading off towards the east. Very few traces of these enclosures now remain. In midst of the avenue lies the flat so-called 'Stone of Sacrifice,' with the rough obelisk of the 'Friar's Heel,' as the most easterly outpost of all, beyond. To the Friar's Heel belongs a legend which gives, by the way, an even more distinguished person than Adam as the builder of Stonehenge. The Devil, according to this story, was the architect, and when he had nearly finished his work, he chuckled to himself that no one would be able to tell how it was done. A wandering friar, however, who had been a witness of it all, remarked, 'That's more than thee can tell,' and thereupon ran away, the Devil flinging one of the stones left over after him.

It only just struck the friar on the heel, and stuck there in the turf, where it stands to this day.

The various stones of which Stonehenge is constructed derive from widely-sundered districts. The outer circle and the five Great Trilithons are said to have been fashioned from stones that came from Marlborough Downs, and the second circle and innermost ellipse belong to a rock formation not known to exist nearer than South Wales. The 'Altar Stone' is different from any of the others, and the circumstance lends some colour to the theory that it, coming from some unknown region, was the original stone fetish brought from a distance by the prehistoric tribe that settled here, around which grew by degrees the subsequent great temple. There are those who will have it that this was a temple of serpent-worshippers; and an argument not altogether unsupported by facts would have us believe that Stonehenge is really a Temple of the Sun. It is a singular accident (if it *is* an accident) that the 'Friar's Heel,' as seen from the centre of the circle, is in exact orientation with the rising sun on the morning of the Longest Day of the year, 21st June. Every year, on this occasion, great crowds of people set out from Salisbury to see sunrise at Stonehenge. There have frequently been as many as three thousand persons present on this occasion. As the spot is nine miles from that cathedral city, and as the sun rises on this date at the early hour of 3.44 A.M., it requires some enthusiasm to rise one's self for the occasion, if indeed the more excellent way is not to sit up all night. Great, therefore, is the disappointment when

SUNRISE AT STONEHENGE.

the morning is misty. If this sunrise phenomenon is not an accident, then Stonehenge, as the Temple of the Sun, is the earliest cathedral in Britain. But, as we have already seen, in these multitudes of guesses at the truth, no one can arrive at the facts, and all we can do is to say frankly, with old Pepys, who was here in 1668, 'God knows what its use was.'

The present historian has waited for the sun to rise here. Arriving at Amesbury village at half-past two in the morning, the street looked and sounded lively with the clustered lights of bicycles and conveyances gathered there; with the ringing of bicycle bells, the sounding of coach-horns, and the talk of those who had come to pay their devoirs to the rising luminary. The village inn was open all night for the needs of travellers journeying to this shrine, and ten minutes was allowed for each person, a policeman standing outside to see that they were duly turned out at the end of that time.

To one who arrived early on the scene, while the Plain remained shrouded in the grayness of the midsummer night, and the rugged stones of Stonehenge yet loomed vague and formless, the scene looking down towards Amesbury was an impressive one. Dimly the ascending white road up to the stones could be discerned by much straining of tired eyes, and along it twinkled brightly the lights of approaching vehicles, now dipping down into a hollow of this miscalled 'Plain,' now toiling slowly and painfully up a corresponding ascent. It is not to be supposed that it was a reverent crowd assembled here. Reverence is not a characteristic of the age, nor are cyclists as a rule, or agricultural folks, or provincials generally, inclined greatly to worship the immeasurably old. And of such this crowd was chiefly composed. It may very pertinently be asked, 'Why, if they don't reverence the place, do they come here at all?' It is a question rather difficult to answer; but probably most people visit it on this occasion as an excuse for being up all night. There would seem to be an idea that there is something dashing and eccentric about such a proceeding which must have its charm for those to whom archæology, or those eternal and unsolvable questions, 'Why was Stonehenge built, and by whom?' have no interest. There were, for instance, two boys on the spot who had come over on their bicycles from Marlborough School, over twenty miles away. Without leave, of course! They hoped to get back as quietly as they had slipped away out of their bedroom windows. Had they any archæological enthusiasm? Not a bit of it, the more especially since it was evident they would have to hurry back before the sun was due to rise.

There were no fewer than fifteen police at Stonehenge, sent on account of the disorderly scenes said to have taken place in previous years. But this crowd was sufficiently quiet. Patiently the throng waited the rising of the sun upon the horizon, and the coming of the shadow of the gnomon-stone across the Stone of Sacrifice. The sky lightened, showing up the tired faces, and transferring the Great Trilithons from the realms of romance to those of commonplace reality. The larks began to trill;

puce- and purple-coloured clouds floated overhead: the brutal staccato notes of a banjo strummed to the air of a music-hall song stale by some three or four seasons; a cyclist struck a match on a sarsen stone; watches were consulted—and the sun refused to rise to the occasion. That is to say, for the twelfth time or so consecutively, according to local accounts, the morning was too cloudy for the sunrise to be seen. So, tired and disappointed, all trooped back to Amesbury, the snapshotters disgusted beyond measure, and breakfasted, or refreshed in various ways, according to individual tastes, at the unholy hour of half-past four o'clock in the morning.

Those who say that Stonehenge will remain a monument to all time speak without a knowledge of the facts. In reality the larger stones are disintegrating: slowly, perhaps, but none the less surely. They are weatherworn, and some of them very decrepit. Frosts have chipped and cracked them, and other extremes of climate have found out the soft places in the sandstone. Also, modern facilities for reaching such out-of-the-way spots as this used to be have brought so many visitors of all kinds here that, in one way and another Stonehenge is bound to suffer. It is now the proper thing for every one who visits Stonehenge to be photographed by the photographer who sits there for that purpose all day long and every day: and although there is no occasion for such insane fury, the picnic parties generally contrive to smash beer and lemonade bottles against the stones until the turf is thickly strewn with broken glass. Modernity also likes to range itself beside the unfathomably ancient, and so when the Automobile Club visited Stonehenge, on Easter Saturday 1899, all the cars and their occupants were photographed beside the stones, to mark so historic an occasion.

XXXI

Away beyond Stonehenge stretches Salisbury Plain, in future to be vulgarised by military camps and manœuvres, and to become an Aldershot on a larger scale, but hitherto a solitude as sublime in its own way as Dartmoor and Exmoor. Dickens gives us his meed of appreciation of this wild country, and finds the boundless prairies of America tame by comparison.

'Now,' he says, writing when on his visit to America, 'a prairie is undoubtedly worth seeing, but more that one may say one *has* seen it, than for any sublimity it possesses in itself. . . . You stand upon the prairie and see the unbroken horizon all round you. You are on a great plain, which is like a sea without water. I am exceedingly fond of wild and lonely scenery, and believe that I have the faculty of being as much impressed by it as any man living. But the prairie fell, by far, short of my preconceived idea. I felt no such emotions as I do in crossing Salisbury Plain. The excessive flatness of the scene makes it dreary, but tame. Grandeur is certainly not its characteristic . . . to say that the sight is a

ANCIENT AND MODERN: MOTOR CARS AT STONEHENGE, EASTER 1899.

landmark in one's existence, and awakens a new set of sensations, is sheer gammon. I would say to every man who can't see a prairie--go to Salisbury Plain, Marlborough Downs, or any of the broad, high, open lands near the sea. Many of them are fully as impressive; and Salisbury Plain is *decidedly* more so.'

Salisbury Plain is the very core and concentrated essence of the wild bleak scenery so characteristic of Wiltshire. An elevated tract of country measuring roughly twenty-four miles from east to west, and sixteen from north to south, and comprising the district between Ludgershall and Westbury, and Devizes and Old Sarum, it is by no means the Plain pictured by strangers, who, misled by that geographical expression, have a mind's-eye picture of it as being quite flat. As a matter of fact, Salisbury Plain is not a bit like that. It is a long series of undulating chalky downs, 'as flat as your hand' if you like, because the hand is anything but flat, and the simile is excellently descriptive of a rolling country that resembles the swelling contours of an outstretched palm. Unproductive, exposed, and lonely, Salisbury Plain opposes even to this day a very effectual barrier against intercourse between north and south or east and west Wiltshire, and was the lurking-place, until even so late as 1839, of highwaymen and footpads, who shared the solitudes with the bustards, and attacked and robbed those travellers whose business called them across the dreary wastes. Many a malefactor has tried his 'prentice hand and learned his business in these wilds, and has, after robbing elsewhere, retired here from pursuit. Salisbury Plain, in short, bred a race of highwaymen who preyed upon the neighbourhood and levied contributions from all the rich farmers and graziers who travelled between the Cathedral City and other parts, and sometimes graduated with such honours that they became Knights of the Road at whose name travellers along the whole length of the Exeter Road would tremble.

Among them was William Davis, the 'Golden Farmer,' whom we have already met at Bagshot. His career was a long one, and was continued, here and in other parts of the country, for forty years. They hanged him, at the age of sixty-nine, in 1689. His most famous exploit was on the borders of the Plain, near Clarendon Park, when he attacked the Duchess of Albemarle, single-handed, and, in the presence of her numerous attendants, tore her diamond rings off her fingers, and would probably have had her watch and money as well, despite her cursing and torrents of full-flavoured abuse, had not the sound of approaching travellers warned him to fly.

'Captain' James Whitney, too, was another desperado who at times made the Plain his headquarters, and harried the Western roads, in the time of William the Third. He was probably a son of the Reverend James Whitney, Rector of Donhead St. Andrews. He raised a troop of highwaymen, and was captured at the close of 1692 after his band had been defeated in battle with the Dragoon Guards. He 'met a most penitent end' at Smithfield.

Then there was Biss, perhaps a descendant of the Reverend Walter Biss, minister of Bishopstrow, near Salisbury, in the reign of Charles the First. Biss the highwayman was hanged at Salisbury in 1695, and was not succeeded by any very distinguished practitioner until Boulter appeared on the scene.

The distinguished Mr. Thomas Boulter was born of poor but dishonest parents at Poulshot, near Devizes, and ran a brief but brilliant and busy course which ended on the gallows outside Winchester. Mr. Boulter's parentage and the deeds that he did form splendid evidence to help bolster up the doctrine of heredity. He came of a very numerous clan of Boulters and Bisses, whose names are even to this day common at Chiverell and Market Lavington, on the Plain. His father rented a grist mill at Poulshot, stole grain for years, and was publicly whipped in Devizes market-place for stealing honey from an old woman's garden. Shortly after that unfortunate incident, in 1775, on returning from Trowbridge, he stole a horse, the property of a Mr. Hall, and riding it over to Andover sold it for £6, although worth at least £15. This injudicious deal aroused the suspicions of the onlookers, so that he was arrested, and being convicted was sentenced to death. But the Boulters and the Bisses made interest for him, so that his sentence was commuted to transportation for fourteen years.

Mrs. Boulter, the wife of this transported felon and the mother of the greater hero, is said to have also suffered a public whipping at the cart's tail, and Isaac Blagden, his uncle, also did a little in the footpad line on Salisbury Plain between the intervals of agricultural labouring. He never attained eminence, having met in an early stage of his career with a sad check while attempting to rob a gentleman near Market Lavington. The traveller drew a pistol and lodged a couple of slugs in his thigh, leaving him bleeding on the highway. Some humane person passing by procured assistance, and had him conveyed to the village. The wound was cured, but he remained a cripple ever afterwards, and being unable to work was admitted into Lavington Workhouse. He was never prosecuted for the attempted crime.

Thomas Boulter, junior, the daring outlaw who shared with Hawkes the title of the 'Flying Highwayman,' and whose name for very many years afterwards was used as a bogey to frighten refractory children, was born in 1748. He worked with his father, the miller, in the grist-mill at Poulshot until 1774, when, his sister having opened a millinery business in the Isle of Wight, he joined her there, and embarked his small capital in a grocery business.

But the business did not flourish. Perhaps it could not be expected to do so in the hands of so roving a blade, for he only gave it a year's perfunctory trial, and then, being pressed for money, set out to find it on the road. He went to Portsmouth, procured two brace of pistols, casting-irons for slugs, and a powder-horn, and, lying by a little while, started in the summer of 1775, on the pretence of paying his mother a visit at Poulshot. Setting out from Southampton, mounted on horseback, he made for the Exeter Road, near 'Winterslow Hut.' In less than a quarter of an hour the Salisbury diligence rewarded his patience and enterprise by coming in sight across the downs. The perspiration oozed out of his every pore, and he was so timid that he rode past the diligence two or three times before he could muster sufficient resolution to pronounce the single word 'Stand!' But at length he found courage in the thought that he must begin, or go home as poor as he came out, and so, turning short round, he ordered the driver to stop, and in less than two minutes had robbed the two passengers of their watches and money, saying that he was much obliged to them, for he was in great want; and so, wishing them a pleasant journey, departed in the direction of Salisbury and Devizes. By the time he reached Poulshot he had robbed three single travellers on horseback and two on foot, and had secured a booty of nearly £40 and seven watches.

This filial visit coming to an end, he returned home to Newport, Isle of Wight, by way of Andover, Winchester, and Southampton. On his way across Salisbury Plain he stopped a post-chaise, several farmers on horseback, one on foot, and two country-women returning from market, going in sight of the last person into Andover, and putting up his horse at the 'Swan,' where he stayed for an hour.

This successful beginning fired our hero for more adventures, and the autumn of the same year found him, equipped with new pistols, a fine suit of clothes, and a horse stolen at Ringwood, making his way to Salisbury, with the intention of riding into the neighbourhood of Exeter before commencing business. But between Salisbury and Blandford he could not resist the temptation of robbing a diligence and a gentleman on horseback, resulting in the rather meagre booty of a gold watch, two guineas, and some silver. He then pushed on through Blandford towards Dorchester, robbing on the way; all in broad daylight. When night was come he thought it prudent to break off from the Exeter Road and lie by at Cerne Abbas until the next afternoon, when he regained the highway near Bridport, very soon finding himself in company with a wealthy grazier who was jogging home in the same direction. The grazier found his companion so sociable that he not only expressed himself as glad of his society, but gossiped at length upon the successful day he had experienced at Salisbury market, where he had sold a number of cattle at an advanced price. He was well known, he said, for carrying the finest beasts to market, and could always command a better price than his neighbours.

Boulter broke in upon this self-satisfied talk with the wish that he had been so lucky in his way of business. Unhappily, repeated misfortunes had at last reduced him to distress, and he had taken to the road for relieving his distresses, and was glad he had had the fortune to fall in with a gentleman who appeared so well able to assist him. Suiting the action to his words, he pulled out a pistol, and begged he might have the pleasure of easing his companion of some of the wealth he had acquired at Salisbury market.

The grazier thought this was a joke and supposed that it was done to frighten him; whereupon Boulter clapped the pistol close to his breast and told him he should not advance a single step until he had delivered his money. In a few minutes his trembling victim had handed over, in bank-notes and cash, nearly £90. His watch, which he seemed to set a value upon for its antiquity, together with some bills of exchange, Boulter returned, and, wishing him good-day, and observing that he should return to London, continued, instead, his journey to Exeter. Altogether, in this trip, he secured a booty of £500, in money and valuables, and spent the winter and these ill-gotten gains among his relatives on Salisbury Plain.

He opened his next campaign in May 1776, having first provided himself with a splendid mare named 'Black Bess,' which he stole from Mr. Peter Delmé's stables at Erle Stoke. This horse, scarce inferior to Turpin's mare of the same name, is indeed supposed to have been a descendant of hers. Starting from Poulshot, he rode to Staines, reaching that place on the second night out. Rising at four o'clock the next morning, he was on the road, in wait for the Western coaches; but he was a prudent man, and at the sight of blunderbusses on their roofs, he concluded that to attack them would be a tempting of Providence. Accordingly, he confined his attentions to the diligences and the post-chaises, and was so active that day that he visited Maidenhead, Hurley, Wokingham, Hartley Row, Whitchurch, and Eversley, reaching Poulshot again the same night with nearly £200, and with the 'Hue and Cry' of five counties at his heels. His exploits on this occasion would not shame the first masters of the art of highway robbery, and the performances of his mare were worthy of her distinguished ancestry. At Hartley Row he called for a bottle of wine, drank a glass himself, and pouring the remainder over a large toast, gave it to his steed, repeating it at Whitchurch and Eversley.

Two months' retirement at Poulshot seemed advisable after this, but during the latter part of the summer and through the autumn he was very busy, his operations extending as far as Bath and Bristol. To give an account of his many robberies would require a long and detailed biography. He did not always meet with travellers willing to resign their purses without a struggle, and on those occasions he generally came off second best; as in the case of the butcher whom he met upon the Plain. Although Boulter held a pistol at the heads of travellers, he never really meant to use it, and it was his boast, at his last hour, that he had never taken life. Perhaps the butcher knew this, for when our friend presented his firearm at his head, and asked him to turn his pockets out, he said, 'I don't get my money so easily as to part with it in that foolish manner. If you rob me, I must go upon the highway myself before I durst go home, and that I'd rather not do.'

What was a good young highwayman, with conscientious scruples about shedding blood, to do under those circumstances? It was an undignified situation, but he retreated from it as best he could, and with the words: 'Good-night, and remember that Boulter is your friend,' disappeared.

In 1777 he took a journey up to York, and was laid by the heels there, escaping the hangman by enlisting, a course then left open to criminals by the Government, which did not tend to bring the Army into better repute. After three days in barracks he deserted, and made the best of his way southwards. Reaching Bristol, he found a fellow-spirit in one James Caldwell, landlord of the 'Ship Inn,' Milk Street, and with him entered upon a new series of robberies. But, first of all, he paid a visit to his relatives at Poulshot, doing some business on the way, and scouring the country round about that convenient retreat. He stopped the diligence again at 'Winterslow Hut,' emptying the pockets of all the passengers, and robbed a Salisbury gentleman near Andover, who, after surrendering his purse, lamented that he had nothing left to carry him home.

'How far have you to go home?' asked Boulter.

'To Salisbury,' said the traveller.

'Then,' rejoined the highwayman, 'here's two-pence, which is quite enough for so short a journey.'

Boulter, according to his biographers, had the light hair and complexion of the Saxon. 'His *bonhomie*, not untinctured with a quiet humour, fascinated and disarmed his victims, who felt that, had he been so disposed, he could have descended upon them like the hammer of Thor.' His companion henceforward, Caldwell, was of a dark complexion and ferocious disposition. Together they visited the Midlands in 1777, and with varying success brought that season to a close, Boulter returning alone to Poulshot for a short holiday from professional cares. Riding on the Plain early one morning, he was surprised to meet a gentlemanly-looking horseman, who looked very hard at him, and who, after passing him about a hundred yards, turned round and pursued him at a gallop. 'Well,' thought Boulter, 'this seems likely to prove a kind of adventure on which I never calculated. I am about to be stopped myself by a gentleman of the road. In what manner will it be necessary to receive the attack.'

The stranger came up rapidly, and whatever his intentions were, merely observed, 'You ride a very fine horse; would you like to sell her?'

'Oh yes,' replied Boulter; 'but for nothing less than fifty guineas.'

'Can she trot and gallop well?'

'She can trot sixteen miles an hour, and gallop twenty, or she would not do for my business,' said Boulter, with a significant look.

By this time the stranger, becoming uneasy, desired to see her paces, probably thinking thus to rid himself of so mysterious a character.

'With all my heart,' rejoined the highwayman, 'you shall see how she goes, but I must first be rewarded for it,' presenting his pistol with the customary demand. That request having been complied with, Boulter wished him good-morning, saying, 'Now, sir, you have seen *my* performance, you shall see the performance of my horse, which I doubt not will perfectly satisfy you'; and putting spur to her, was soon but a distant speck upon the Plain, leaving the stranger to bewail his foolish curiosity.

The winter of 1777 and the spring of 1778 were employed by Boulter and Caldwell in scouring Salisbury Plain and the neighbouring country. A reward had long been offered for the apprehension of the robber who infested the district, and the appearance of a confederate now alarmed Salisbury so greatly that private persons began to advertise in the local papers their readiness to supplement this sum. A public subscription, amounting to twenty guineas, was also raised at Devizes, so that there was every inducement to the peasantry to make a capture. Yet, strange to say, no one, either private or official persons, laid a hand on them, even though Boulter appears to have been identified with the daring horseman who robbed every one crossing the Plain. The following advertisement appeared 10th January 1778:—

WHEREAS divers robberies have been lately committed on the road from Devizes to Salisbury, and also near the town of Devizes: and as it is strongly suspected that one Boulter, with an accomplice, are the persons concerned in these robberies, a reward of thirty guineas is offered for apprehending and bringing to justice the said Boulter, and ten guineas for his accomplice, over and above the reward allowed by Act of Parliament:—to be paid, on conviction, at the Bank in Devizes. If either of these persons are taken in any distant part of the country, reasonable charges will also be allowed. Boulter is about five feet eleven inches high, stout made, light hair, crooked nose, brownish complexion, and about thirty years of age. His accomplice, about five feet nine inches high, thin made, long favoured, black hair, and is said to be about twenty-five years of age.

This publicity did not hinder their enterprises, and speaking of Boulter, a little later, the *Salisbury Journal* says: 'The robberies he has committed about Salisbury, the Plain, Romsey, and Southampton, and the several roads to London, are innumerable.'

But what local law and order could not accomplish was effected at Birmingham, to which town the confederates had made a journey in the spring of 1778, for the purpose of selling some of the jewellery and watches they had accumulated. Boulter had approached a Jew dealer on the subject, and was arrested, together with Caldwell, and thrown into Birmingham Prison. They were sent thence to Clerkenwell, from which, having already secured by bribery a jeweller's saw and cut through his irons, he escaped, with two other prisoners, carrying the irons away with him, and hanging them in triumph on a whitethorn bush at St. Pancras. With consummate impudence he took lodgings two doors away from Clerkenwell Prison, and, procuring a new outfit, set off down to Dover, to take ship across the Channel. But, unfortunately for him, the country was on the eve of a war with France, and an embargo had been laid upon all shipping. He could not even secure a small sailing-boat. Hurrying off to Portsmouth, he found the same difficulty, and could not even get across to the Isle of Wight. Thence to Bristol, haunted with a constant fear of being arrested; but not a single vessel was leaving that port. Then it occurred to him that the desolate Isle of Portland was the most likely hiding-place. Setting out from Bristol, he reached Bridport, and went to an inn to refresh himself and his horse. When he asked what he could have for dinner, he was told there was a family ordinary just ready. He accordingly sat down at table, beside the landlord and three gentlemen, one of whom eyed him with a searching scrutiny, until, becoming fully satisfied that this was none other than Boulter, the escaped prisoner, he beckoned the landlord out of the room, and reminded him of the duty and necessity which lay upon them of securing so notorious an offender. The landlord then returned to the dining-room and desired Boulter to accompany him to an adjoining parlour, where he revealed to him the perilous state of affairs; but added, 'As you have never done me an injury, I wish you no harm, so just pay your reckoning, and be off as quick as you can.'

Boulter bade him tell the strangers that they were totally mistaken, that he was a London rider (that is to say, a commercial traveller), and that his name was White; but having no wish to be the cause of a disturbance in his house, he would take his advice and go on his way.

The landlord went back to his guests, and Boulter got on his horse with all possible expedition. Once fairly seated in the saddle, a single application of the spur would have launched him beyond the reach of these hungry pursuers, nor in such an emergency as this would his pistol be harmlessly pointed against those who thus sought to earn the rewards offered for his capture. Alas! he had but placed his foot in the stirrup when out rushed the false landlord and his guests. They secured him, and being handed over to the authorities, he was lodged in Dorchester Gaol. He was arraigned at Winchester with Caldwell (who had been removed from London) on 31st July, and both being found guilty, they were hanged at Winchester, 19th August 1778.

XXXII

Soon after those two comrades had met their end, there arose a highway-woman to trouble the district. This was Mary Sandall, of Baverstock, a young woman of twenty-four years of age, who had borrowed a pair of pistols and a suit of his clothes from the blacksmith of Quidhampton, and, bestriding a horse, set out one day in the spring of 1779, and meeting Mrs. Thring, of North Burcombe, robbed her of two shillings and a black silk cloak. Mrs. Thring went home and raised an alarm, with the result that Mary Sandall was captured, and committed for trial at the next assizes. Although there seems to have been some idea that this was a practical joke, the authorities were thick-headed persons who had heard too much of the real thing to be patient with an amateur highway-woman, and so they sentenced Mary Sandall to death in due form, although she was afterwards respited as a matter of course.

William Peare was the next notability of the roads, but it is not certain that he was the one who stopped Mr. Jeffery, of Yateminster, on his way home from Weyhill, 9th October 1780, and knocking him off his horse, robbed him of £500 in bank-notes and £37 in coin. It was the same unknown, doubtless, who during the same week robbed a Mrs. Turner, of Upton Scudamore, of £45, in broad daylight. He was a 'genteelly-dressed' stranger. Making a low bow, he requested her money, and that within sight of many people working in the fields, who concluded, from his polite manners, that he was a friend of the lady.

William Peare was only twenty-three years of age when he was executed, 19th August 1783. His first important act was the robbing of the Chippenham coach on the 2nd of February 1782. Captured, and lodged in Gloucester Gaol, he escaped on the 19th of April, and began a series of the most daring highway robberies. On the 8th of February 1783 he stopped the Salisbury diligence just beyond St. Thomas's Bridge, smashed the window, and fired a shot into the coach, terrifying the lady and gentleman who were the only two passengers, so that they at once gave up their purses. He then went on to Stockbridge, where he stopped a diligence full of military officers: but finding the occupants prepared to fight for the military chest they were escorting, hurried off. After many other crimes in the West, he was captured in the act of undermining a bank at Stroud, in Gloucestershire. He was tried and sentenced at Salisbury, and executed at Fisherton, going to the gallows with the customary nosegay, which remained tightly held in his hand when his body was cut down. A set of verses, purporting to be by his sweetheart, was published that year, lamenting his untimely end:

> For me he dared the dangerous road,
> My days with goodlier fare to bless;
> He took but from the miser's hoard,
> From them whose station needed less.

Highwaymen continued numerous at the dawn of the nineteenth century, as may be judged from the executions at Fisherton Gaol, or on the scenes of their misdeeds, that continued to afford a spectacle for the mob. For highway robbery alone one man was hanged in 1806, one in 1816, two in 1817, and two in 1824; while three were sentenced to fifteen years' transportation in 1839 for a similar offence near Imber, in the very centre of the Plain.

The spot was Gore Cross, a solitary waste; time and date, seven o'clock on the evening of 21st October 1839. Upon this wilderness entered Mr. Matthew Dean, of Imber, returning on horseback from Devizes Fair, when he was suddenly set upon by four men, dragged off his horse, and robbed of £20 in notes of the North Wilts Bank, and £3 : 10s. in coin. The gang then made off, but Mr. Dean followed them on foot. On the way he met Mr. Morgan, of Chitterne; but being afraid that the men carried pistols they decided to get more help before pursuing them farther. So they called on a Mr. Hooper, who joined the chase on horseback, armed with a double-barrelled gun. Meeting a Mr. Sainsbury, he accompanied the party, and, pressing on, they presently came in sight of the men. One ran away for some miles at a great pace, and they could not overtake him until about midway between Tilshead and Imber, where he fell down and lay still on the grass. His pursuers thought this to be a feint, and were afraid to seize him, so they continued the chase of the other three, who were eventually captured. The next day the body of the unfortunate

HIGHWAY ROBBERY MONUMENT AT IMBER

man was found where he had fallen, quite dead. He had died from heart disease. An inquest was held on him, and the curious verdict of *felo-de-se* returned, according to the law which holds a person a suicide who commits an unlawful act, the consequence of which is his death. Two memorial stones mark the spot where the robbery took place and the spot, two miles distant, where the man fell.

The times were still dangerous for wayfarers here, for a few weeks later, on the night of 16th November, between nine and ten o'clock P.M., a Mr. Richard Brown, of Little Pannel, driving a horse and cart, was attacked by two footpads near Gore Cross Farm. One seized the horse, while the other gave him two tremendous blows on the head with a bludgeon, which almost deprived him of his senses. Recovering, he knocked the fellow down with his fist. Then the two jumped into the cart and robbed him of ten shillings, running away when he called for help, and leaving him with his purse containing £14 in notes and gold.

With this incident the story of highway robbery on Salisbury Plain comes to an end, and a very good thing too.

XXXIII

If you want to know exactly what kind of a road the Exeter Road is between Salisbury and Bridport, a distance of twenty-two miles, I think the sketch facing page 238 will convey the information much better than words alone. It is just a repetition of those bleak seventeen miles between Andover and Salisbury—only 'more so.' More barren and hillier than the Andover to Salisbury section, and less romantically wild than the rugged stretches between Blandford,

Dorchester, and Bridport, it is a weariness to man and beast. Buffeted by the winds which shriek across the rolling downs, or nipped by the keen airs of these altitudes, old-time travellers up to London or

WHERE THE ROBBER FELL DEAD.

down to Exeter dreaded the passage, and prepared themselves, accordingly, at Bridport or at Salisbury, while exhausted nature was recruited at the several inns which found their existence abundantly justified in those old times.

Passing through West Harnham, a suburb of Salisbury, the road immediately begins to climb the downs, descending, however, in three miles to the charming little village of Coombe Bissett, in the water-meadows of the Wiltshire Avon, which runs prettily beside the road. An ancient church, old thatched barns standing on stone staddles whose feet are in the stream, bridges across the water, and the inevitable downs closing in the view, make one of the rare picturesque compositions to be found along this dreary stretch of country.

Make much, wayfarer, of Coombe Bissett. Linger there, soothe your soul with its rural graces before proceeding; for the road immediately leaves this valley of the Avon, and the next bend discloses the unfenced rolling downs, going in a mile-long rise, and so continuing, with a balance in the matter of gradients against the traveller going westwards, all the way to Blandford.

At eight miles from Salisbury is situated the old 'Woodyates Inn,' placed in this lonely situation, far removed from any village, in the days when the coaching traffic made the custom of travellers worth obtaining. It was in those days thought that after travelling eight miles the passengers by coach or post-chaise would want refreshments. It was a happy and well-founded thought; and if all tales be true, the prowess of our great-grandfathers as trenchermen left nothing to be desired—nor anything remaining in the larder when they had done.

The curious, on the lookout for this old coaching inn, will scarcely recognise it when seen, for it has

been garnished and painted, and rechristened of late years by the title of the 'Shaftesbury Arms.' But there it is, and portions of it may be found to date back to the old times.

It was given the name of 'Woodyates' from its position standing at the entrance to the wooded district of Cranborne Chase; the name meaning 'Wood-gates.' It also stands on the border-line dividing the counties of Wilts and Dorset.

Bokerley Dyke, a prehistoric boundary consisting of a bank and ditch, intersects the road as you approach the inn, and goes meandering over the downs among the gorse and bracken. Built, no doubt, more than fifteen hundred years ago by savages, solely with the aid of their hands and pointed sticks, it has outlasted many monuments of costly stones and marbles, and when civilisation comes to an end some day, like the blown-out flame of a candle, it will still be there, with the existing, but more recent, Roman road still beside it. That road goes across the open country like a causeway, or a slightly raised railway embankment.

The Dyke may have sheltered the fugitive Duke of Monmouth on his flight in 1685. The reading of that melancholy story of how the handsome and gay Duke of Monmouth, a haggard fugitive from Sedgemoor Fight, accompanied by his friend, Lord Grey, and another, left their wearied horses near this spot, and, disguising themselves as peasants, set out for the safe hiding-places of the New Forest, only to fall prisoners to James's scouts, paints the road and the downs with an impasto of tragedy. All the countryside was being searched for him, and watchers were stationed on the hills, looking down upon this open country where the movement of a rabbit almost might be noted from afar. So he doubtless skulked along in the shadow of the Dyke from the shelter of Cranborne Chase down to Woodlands, where he was caught, under the shadow of a tree still standing, called Monmouth Ash.

Scattered all around are the inevitable barrows. The industry of a bygone generation of antiquaries has explored them all. Pick and shovel have scattered the ashes and the cinerary urns of the Britons or Saxons who were buried here, and the only relics likely to be found by any other ghouls are the discs of lead deposited by Sir Richard Colt Hoare, or W. Cunnington, with the initials 'R. C. H. 1815,' or some such date; or, 'Opened by W. Cunnington 1804' on them.

George the Third always used to change horses at 'Woodyates Inn' when journeying to or from Weymouth, and the room built for his use on those occasions is still to be seen, with its outside flight of steps. When the coaches were taken off the road, the inn became for a time the training establishment of William Day.

The road near this old inn is the real scene of the Ingoldsby legend of the *Dead Drummer*, and not Salisbury Plain, on 'one of the rises' where

> An old way-post shewed
> Where the Lavington road
> Branched off to the left from the one to Devizes.

THE EXETER ROAD, NEAR 'WOODYATES INN.'

It was on Thursday, 15th June 1786, that two sailors, paid off from H.M.S. *Sampson*, at Plymouth, and walking up to London, came to this spot. Their names were Gervase (or Jarvis) Matcham, and John Shepherd. Near the 'Woodyates Inn' they were overtaken by a thunderstorm, in which Matcham startled his companion by showing extraordinary marks of horror and distraction, running about, falling on his knees, and imploring mercy of some invisible enemy. To his companion's questions he answered that he saw several strange and dismal spectres, particularly one in the shape of a female, towards which he advanced, when it instantly sank into the earth, and a large stone rose up in its place. Other large stones also rolled upon the ground before him, and came dashing against his feet. He confessed to Shepherd that, about seven years previously, he had enlisted as a soldier at Huntingdon, and shortly afterwards was sent out from that town in company with a drummer-boy, seventeen years of age, named Jones, son of a sergeant in the regiment, who was in charge of some money to be paid away. They quarrelled because the lad refused to return and drink at a public-house on the Great North Road which they had just passed, four miles from Huntingdon. Matcham knocked him down, cut his throat, and taking the money (six guineas) made off to London, leaving the body by the roadside. He now declared that, with this exception, he had never in his life broken the law, and that, before the moment of committing this crime, he had not the least design of injuring the deceased, who had given him no other provocation than ill-language. But from that hour he had been a stranger to peace of mind; his crime was always present to his imagination, and existence seemed at times an insupportable burden. He begged his companion to deliver him into the hands of Justice in the next town they should reach. That was Salisbury. He was imprisoned there, brought to trial, found guilty, and hanged.

Barham in his legend of the *Dead Drummer* has taken many liberties with the facts of the case, both as regards place and names, and makes the scene of the murderer's terror identical with the site of the crime, which he (for purely literary purposes) places on Salisbury Plain, instead of the Great North Road, between Buckden and Alconbury.

XXXIV

Three more inns were situated beside the road between this point and Blandford in the old days. Of them, two, the 'Thorney Down Inn,' and the 'Thickthorn Inn' (romantic and shuddery names!), have disappeared, while the remaining one,—the 'Cashmoor Inn'—formerly situated between the other two, ekes out a much less important existence than of old, as a wayside 'public.'

Then comes a village—the first one since Coombe Bissett was passed, fifteen miles behind, and so more than usually welcome. A pretty village, too, Tarrant Hinton by name, lying in a hollow, with its little

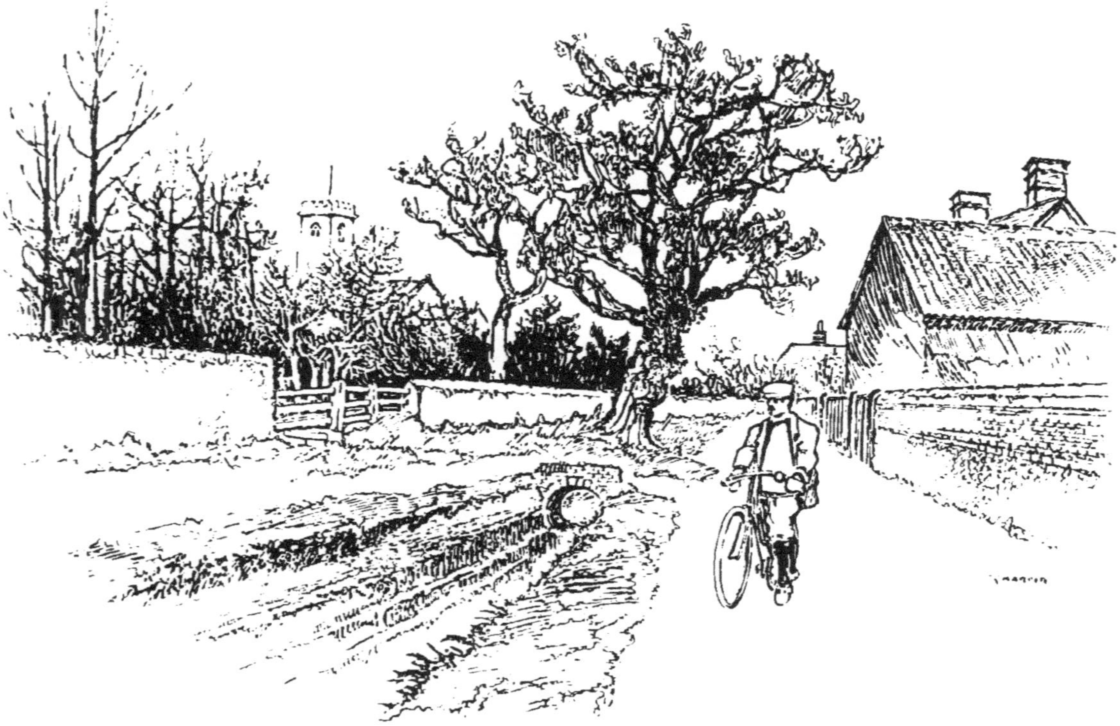

TARRANT HINTON.

street of cottages, along a road running at right angles to the Exeter highway, with its church tower peeping above the orchards and thick coppices, and a sparkling stream flowing down from the hillside. In this and other respects, it bears a striking similarity to Middle and Over Wallop.

The quiet, not to say sleepy, Dorsetshire villager who, lounging at the bend of the road, replies to your query by saying that this is 'Tarnt Hinton,' is the peaceable descendant of very desperate and bloody-minded men, and the like circumstances that, a mere hundred years ago, rendered them savages, would do the same by him, were they revived. The peasantry are what the law and social conditions make them. Oppress the sturdy rustic and you render him a brutal and resentful rebel, who, having an unbroken spirit, will give trouble. Treat him fairly, and he will live a life of quiet industry, tempered by gossipy evenings in the village 'pub.'; and although he will never rise to be the mincing Strephon imagined by the eighteenth-century poets of rurality, he will raise gigantic potatoes, and cultivate flowers for the local Horticultural Society, and do nothing more tragical in all his life than the sticking of the domestic porker, or the twisting of a fowl's neck.

The civilising of the rustic in these parts dates from the disfranchising of Cranborne Chase in 1830. The Chase, which took its name from the town of Cranborne, eight miles distant from this spot, was originally a vast deer-forest, extending far into Hants, Wilts, and Dorset. The great western highway entered it at Salisbury and did not pass out of its bounds until Blandford was reached; while Shaftesbury to the north, and Wimborne to the south, marked its extent in another direction. Belonging anciently to great feudal lords or to the Sovereign, it was Crown property from the time of Edward the Fourth to the reign of James the First. James delighted in killing the buck here, but that Royal prig granted the Chase to the Earl of Pembroke, from whom, shorn of its oppressive laws, it has descended to Lord Rivers; while the Earl of Shaftesbury also owns great tracts of woodlands here. But, singularly enough, that part of the Chase which still retains the wildest and densest aspect lies quite away from Cranborne, and in the county of Wilts, around Tollard Royal. The nature of the country and the character of the soil must needs always keep this vast tract wild, and, in an agricultural sense, unproductive. Game will always abound here in the thickets, and indeed the weird-looking hill-top plantations, called by the rustics 'hats of trees,' are especially planted as cover, wherever the country is open and unsheltered.

The severity of the laws which governed a Chase and punished deer-stealers was simply barbarous. Cranborne had its courts and Chase Prison where offenders and deer-stealers were punished by mutilation, imprisonment, or fine, according to the crime, the status of the offender, or the comparative state of civilisation of the period in which the offence was committed. But whether the punishment for stealing deer was the striking off of a hand, or imprisonment in a noisome dungeon, or merely being mulcted in a larger or smaller sum, there were always those who unlawfully killed the buck in these romantic glades. Sometimes, for the devilment of it, the dashing young blades of the countryside—sons of the squires and others—would hunt the deer.

'From four to twenty assembled in the evening, dressed in cap and jack and quarter-staff, with dogs and nets. Having set the watchword for the night and agreed whether they should stand or run if they should meet the keepers, they proceeded to the Chase. set their nets, and let slip their dogs to drive the deer into the nets; a man standing at each net, to strangle the deer as soon as they were entangled. Frequent desperate and bloody battles took place; the keepers, and sometimes the hunters, were killed.'

Other law-breakers were of a humbler stamp, and ferocious enough to murder keepers at sight. Thus, in 1738, a keeper named Tollerfield was murdered on his way home from Fontmell Church: and another at Fernditch, near 'Woodyates Inn.' For the latter crime a man named Wheeler was convicted, and suffered the extreme penalty of the law; his body being hanged in chains at the scene of the murder. His friends, however, in the course of a few nights cut the body down, and threw it into a very deep well, some distance away. The weight of the irons caused it to sink, and it was not discovered until long afterwards.

One of the most exciting of these encounters between the deer-stealers and the keepers took place on the night of 16th December 1781. Chettle Common, away at the back of the 'Cashmoor Inn,' was the scene of this battle. The stealers, assembling in disguise at

Pimperne, marched up the road through the night, and headed by a Sergeant of Dragoons, then quartered at Blandford, poured through the Thickthorn Toll-gate, armed with weapons called 'swindgels,' which appear to have been hinged cudgels, like flails. It would seem that the object of this expedition was the bludgeoning of a few keepers, rather than the stealing of deer. At any rate, the keepers expected them, and armed with sticks and hangers, awaited the attack. The fight was by no means a contemptible one, for in the result one keeper was killed and several disabled, while the stealers were so badly knocked about that the whole expedition surrendered, together with the Sergeant of Dragoons, who had a hand sliced off at the wrist by a hanger. The hand was subsequently buried, with military honours, in Pimperne churchyard.

Leader and followers alike were committed to Dorchester Gaol, and were eventually sentenced to seven years' penal servitude, reduced to a nominal term, in consideration of the severe wounds from which they were suffering. One wonders how far mercy, and to what extent the wish not to be at the expense of medically attending the prisoners, influenced this decision. As for the Dr. Jameson of this raid, he retired from the Dragoons on half-pay, and, coming to London, set up shop as a dealer in game and poultry!

Ten years later, a keeper killed a stealer, and another murderous encounter took place on 7th December 1816 near Tarrant Gunville, at a gate in the woods which the melodramatic instincts of the peasantry have named 'Bloody Shard,' while the wood itself is known as 'Blood-way Coppice.'

Cranborne Chase was also at this time a haunt of smugglers, who found its tangled recesses highly convenient for storing their 'Free Trade' merchandise on its way up from the sea-coast. Whether or not the original 'Wiltshire moonrakers' belonged to the Wilts portion of the Chase or to some other part of the county, tradition does not say.

That Wiltshire folk are called 'moonrakers' is generally known, and it is usually supposed that they obtained this name for stupidity, according to the story which tells how a party of travellers crossing a bridge in this county observed a number of rustics raking in the stream in which the great yellow harvest-moon was shining. Asked what they were doing, the reply was that they were trying to rake 'that cheese' out of the water. The travellers went on their way, laughing at the idiotcy of the yokels. One tale, however, only holds good until the other is told. The facts seem to be that the rustics were smugglers who were raking in the river for the brandy-kegs they had deposited there in the gray of the morning, and that the 'travellers' were really revenue-officers; those 'gangers,' or 'preventive men' who were employed to check the smuggling which was rife a hundred years ago. It may be thought that the seaside was the only place where smuggling could be carried on, but a moment's reflection will show that the goods had to be conveyed inshore for inland customers. Smuggling, in fact, was so extensive, and brought to such a perfection of system that forwarding agents were established everywhere. Kegs of spirits, being bulky, were hidden for the day in ponds and watercourses, wherever possible, and removed at night for another stage towards their destination, being deposited in a similar hiding-place at the break of day, and so forth until they reached their consignees. Thus the 'moonrakers' by this explanation are acquitted of being monumental simpletons, at the expense of losing their reputation in another way. But everyone smuggled, or received or purchased smuggled goods, in those times, and no one was thought the worse for it.

XXXV

At the distance of a mile up the bye-road from Tarrant Hinton, in Eastbury Park, still stands in a lonely position the sole remaining wing of the once-famed Eastbury House, one of those immense palaces which the flamboyant noblemen and squires of a past era loved to build. Comparable for size and style with Blenheim and Stowe, and built like them by the ponderous Vanbrugh, the rise and fall of Eastbury were as dramatic as the building and destruction of Canons, the seat of the 'princely Chandos' at Edgware. Of Canons, however, no stone remains, while at Eastbury a wing and colonnade are left, standing sinister, sundered and riven, the melancholy relics of a once proud but hospitable mansion.

Eastbury was begun on a scale of princely magnificence by George Dodington, a former Lord of the Admiralty, who, having presumably made some fine pickings in that capacity, determined to spend them on becoming a patron of the Arts and an entertainer of literary men, after the fashion of an age in which painters were made to fawn upon the powerful, and poets to sing their praises in the blankest of blank verse. Every rich person had his henchmen among the followers of the Muses, and they were petted or scolded, indulged or kept on the chain, just as the humour of the patron at the moment decreed. Unfortunately, however, for this eminently eighteenth-century ambition of George Dodington, he died before he could finish his building. All his worldly goods went to his grand-nephew, George Bubb, son of his brother's daughter, who had married a Weymouth apothecary named Jeremias Bubb. Already, under the patronage of his uncle, a member of Parliament, and an influential person, George on coming into this property assumed the name of Dodington; perhaps also because the obvious nickname of 'Silly Bubb' by which he was known might thereby become obsolete.

George Bubb Dodington, as he was now known, immediately stopped the works on his uncle's palace, and thus the unfinished building remained gaunt and untenanted from 1720 to 1738. Then, as suddenly as the building was stopped, work was resumed again. The vast sum of £140,000 was spent on the completion. Tapestries, gilding, marbles, everything of the most costly and ornate character was employed, and the grounds which had been newly laid out eighteen years before, and in the interval allowed to subside into a wilderness, were set in order again. The reason of this sudden activity was that Dodington had become infected with that same 'Patron' mania which had caused his uncle to lay the foundation stones of these marble halls. He was at this period forty-seven years of age, and in those years had filled many posts in the Government, and about the rival Whig and Tory Courts of the King and the Prince of Wales. Scheming and intriguing from one party to the other, he had always been ambitious of influence, and now that even greater accumulations of wealth had come to him, he set up as the host of birth, beauty, and intellect in these Dorsetshire wilds.

The gossips of the time have left us a picture of the man. Fat, ostentatious, extravagant, with the love of glitter and colour of a barbarian, he was yet a wit of repute, and had undoubtedly some learning. He possessed, besides, a considerable share of shrewdness. If he lent £5000 to Frederick, Prince of Wales, and never got it back, we are not to suppose that he ever expected to be repaid. That was, no doubt, regarded as practically an entrance-fee to the exalted companionship of a prince of whom it was written, when he came to an untimely end :—

But since it's Fred who is dead, there's no more to be said.

That same Fred thought *himself* the clever man when he remarked 'Dodington is reckoned clever, but I have borrowed £5000 of him which he will never see again'; but Dodington doubtless imagined the sum to have been well laid out; which, indeed, would have been the case had not the prince died early. Mæcenas was, in fact, working for a title, and this was then regarded as the ready way to such a goal. They say the same idea prevails in our own happy times; but that £5000 would not go far towards the realisation of the object. But, be that as it may, Dodington did not win to the Peerage as Lord Melcombe until 1761, and as he died in the succeeding year, his enjoyment of the ermine was short. As, however, the working towards an object and its anticipation are always more enjoyable than the attainment of the end, he is perhaps not to be regarded with pity, or thought a failure.

One who partook of his hospitality at Eastbury, and did not think the kindness experienced there a sufficient reason for silence as to his host's eccentricities and failings, has given us some entertaining stories. The State bed of the gross but witty Dodington at Eastbury was covered with gold and silver embroidery; a gorgeous sight, but closer inspection revealed the fact that this splendour had been contrived at the expense of his old coats and breeches, whose finery had been so clumsily converted that the remains of the pocket-holes were clearly visible. 'His vast figure,' continues this reminiscencing friend, 'was always arrayed in gorgeous brocades, and when he paid his court at St. James's, he approached to kiss the Queen's hand, decked in an embroidered suit of silk, with lilac waistcoat and breeches; the latter in the act of kneeling down, forgot their duty and broke loose from their moorings in a very indecorous and uncourtly manner.' That must have been a sore blow to the dignity of one who possessed, as we are told, 'the courtly and profound devotion of a Spaniard towards women, with the ease and gaiety of a Frenchman to men.'

Rolling down the Exeter Road, from his London mansion, or from his suburban retreat of 'La Trappe,' at Hammersmith, in his gilded, old-fashioned chariot, he gathered a variety of literary men at what Young calls 'Pierian Eastbury.' Johnson, sick of the Chesterfields and the whole gang of literary patrons, scornfully refused Dodington's proffered friendship; but Fielding, Thomson, Bentley, Cumberland, Young, Voltaire, and others were not slow to revel in these more or less Arcadian delights. Christopher Pitt wrote to Young, congratulating him on his stay here:—

> Where with your Dodington retired you sit,
> Charmed with his flowing Burgundy and wit:
> Where a new Eden in the wild is found,
> And all the seasons in a spot of ground.

While Thomson, moved to it by the Burgundy or the more potent punch, has celebrated palace and park in his *Autumn*.

Dodington had either no stomach for fighting, or else was a good fellow beyond the common run, as the following affair proves. Eastbury marches with Cranborne Chase, and one day the Ranger found one of Dodington's keepers with his dogs in a part of the Chase called Burseystool Walk. The keeper was warned that if he was found there again, his dogs would be shot and himself prosecuted; but despite this warning he was found near the same spot a few days later, when the Ranger, having a gun in his hand, put his threat into execution and shot the three dogs as they were drinking in a pool, with their heads close together, in one of the Ridings. Dodington, in a first outburst of fury, sent a challenge to the Ranger over this affair, and the Ranger bought a sword and sent a friend to call on the challenger to fix time and place for the encounter: but by that time Dodington had thought better of it, and instead of making arrangements to shed the enemy's gore, invited both him and his friend to dinner. They met and had a jovial time together, and the sword remained unspotted.

On Dodington's death his estates passed to Earl Temple, who could not afford to keep up the vast place. He accordingly offered an income of £200 a year to anyone who would live at Eastbury and keep it in repair. No one came forward to accept these terms; and so, after the pictures, objects of art, and the furniture had been sold, the great house was pulled down, piecemeal, in 1795, with the exception of this solitary fragment.

There is room for much reflection in Eastbury Park to-day, by the crumbling archway with the two large fir-trees growing between the joints of its masonry; by the remaining wing, or the foundations of the rest of the vanished house, which can still be distinctly traced in the grass during dry summers. The stories of 'Haunted Eastbury' and of the headless coachman and his four-in-hand are dying out, but the panelled room in which Doggett, Earl Temple's fraudulent steward, shot himself is still to be seen.

Doggett had embezzled money, and when discovered found this the only way out of his trouble.

When the church of Tarrant Gunville, just outside the Park gates, was rebuilt in 1845 the workmen found his body, the legs tied together with a yellow silk ribbon which was as bright and fresh as the day it was tied.

XXXVI

Returning to the road at Tarrant Hinton, a steep hill leads up to the wild downs again, with a corresponding descent in three miles into the village of Pimperne whose chief part is situated in the same manner, along a byeway at a right angle to the coach-road. There is a battered cross on an open space near the church, and the church itself has been severely restored. Christopher Pitt was Rector of Pimperne, and it requires no great stretch of imagination to conjure up a vision of him pacing the road to Eastbury, and composing laudatory verses on Dodington and his 'flowing wit'; rendered, perhaps, the more eloquent by anticipations of the flow of Burgundy already quoted. He died in 1748, fourteen long years, alas! before the wine had ceased to flow at that Pierian spot.

From this haunt of the Muses it is two miles to the town of Blandford Forum, whose name it is sad to be obliged to record is nowadays shamefully docked to 'Blandford,' although the market, whence the distinctive appellation of 'Forum' derived, is still in existence.

One comes downhill into Blandford, all the way from Pimperne, and it remains a standing wonder how the old coachmen managed to drive their top-heavy conveyances through the steep and narrow streets by which the town is entered from London, without upsetting and throwing the 'outsides' through the first-floor windows.

If the outskirts of Blandford town are of so mediæval a straitness, the chief streets of it are spacious indeed and lined with houses of a classic breadth and dignity, as classicism was understood in the days of George the Second, when the greater part of the town was burnt down and rebuilt. One needs not to be in love with classic, or debased classic, architecture to love Blandford. The town is stately, and with a thoroughly urban air, although its streets are so quiet, clean, and well-ordered. Civilisation without its usual accompaniments of rush and crowded pavements would seem to be the rule of Blandford. You can actually stand in the street and admire the architectural details of its houses without being run over or hustled off the pavement. In short, Blandford can be *seen*, and not, like crowded towns, glimpsed with intermittent and alternate glances at the place and at the traffic, for fear of jostling or being jostled.

Who, for instance, really *sees* London. You can stand in Hyde Park and see that, or in St. Paul's and observe all the details of it; but does anyone ever really *see* Cheapside, Fleet Street, or the Strand, when walking? The only way to make acquaintance with these thoroughfares is to ride on the outside of an omnibus, where it is possible to give an undivided attention to anything else than the crowds that throng the pavements.

The progress of Blandford seems to have been quietly arrested soon after its rebuilding in 1731, and so it remains typical of that age, without being actually decayed. So far, indeed, is it from decay that it is a cheerful and prosperous, though not an increasing, town. Red moulded and carved brick frontages to the houses prevail here, and dignity is secured by the tall classic tower of the church, which, although not in itself entirely admirable, and although the stone of it is of an unhealthy green tinge, is not unpleasing, placed to advantage closing the view at one end of the broad market-place, instead of being aligned with the street.

Most things in Blandford date back to 'the fire,' which forms a red-letter day in the story of the town. This may well be understood when it is said that only forty houses were left when the flames had done their worst, and that fourteen persons were burnt, while others died from grief, or shock, or injuries received. Blandford has been several times destroyed by fire. In Camden's time it was burned down by accident, but was rebuilt soon after in a handsome and substantial form. Again in 1677 and in 1713 the place was devastated in the same manner. The memorable fire of 1731 began at a soap-boiler's shop in the centre of the town.

A pump, placed in a kind of shrine under the

BLANDFORD.

churchyard wall, bears an inscription recounting this terrible happening:—

In remembrance
Of God's dreadful visitation by Fire,
Which broke out the 4th of June, 1731,
and in a few Hours not only reduced the
Church, but almost the whole Town, to Ashes,
Wherein 14 Inhabitants perished,
But also two adjacent Villages;
And
In grateful Acknowledgement of the
Divine Mercy,
That has since raised this Town,
Like the Phœnix from its Ashes,
To its present flourishing and beautiful State;
and to prevent,
By a timely Supply of Water,
(With God's Blessing) the fatal
Consequences of Fire hereafter:
This Monument
Of that dire Disaster, and Provision
Against the like, is humbly erected
By
John Bastard
A considerable Sharer
In the great Calamity,
1760.

Between 1760 and 1762 Gibbon, the historian of the *Decline and Fall of the Roman Empire*, was constantly in the neighbourhood of Blandford, camping on the downs which surround the town, and enjoying all the pomp and circumstance which may have belonged to his position as a Captain of Hants Militia.

Of these amateur soldierings he speaks as a

'wandering life of military service,' a very amusing view of what everybody else but that pompous historian regarded as mere picnics.

But Gibbon, although his person was not precisely that of an ideal military commander, and although the awkward squads he accompanied were not easily comparable with the legions of old Rome, affected to believe that the military knowledge he thus acquired among the hills and woodlands of Hants and Dorset was of the greatest use in helping him to understand the strategic feats of Cæsar and Hannibal in Britain or across the Alps. Let us smile!

In after years, when living at Lausanne, amid the eternal hills and mountains of Switzerland, he looked back upon those days with regret, alike for the good company of his brother officers, the jovial nights at the 'Crown' in 'pleasant, hospitable Blandford,' and for the interference those happy times caused to his studies; when, instead of burning the midnight oil, he drank deeply of the two-o'clock-in-the-morning punch-bowl.

Many of Blandford's natives have risen to more than local eminence. Latest among her distinguished sons is Alfred Stevens, that fine artist who designed the Wellington Monument in St. Paul's Cathedral, as yet, unhappily, incomplete. He came into contact with governments and red-tape, and broken in spirit and in health by disappointments, died in 1875. A tablet on the wall of his birthplace in Salisbury Street records the fact that he was born in 1817.

TOWN BRIDGE, BLANDFORD.

XXXVII

Sixteen and a quarter miles of very varied road brought the old coachmen with steaming horses clattering from Blandford into Dorchester, past the villages of Winterborne Whitchurch, Milborne St. Andrew, and the village of Piddletown, which is by no means a town, and never was.

It is a long, long rise out of Blandford, past tree-shaded Bryanstone and over the Town Bridge, to the crest of Charlton Downs, a mile out; where, looking back, the town is seen lying in a wooded hollow almost surrounded by park-like trees in dense clumps—the woods of Bryanstone. From this point of vantage it is clearly seen how Blandford is entered downhill from east or west.

Very hilly, very open, very white and hot and dusty in summer, and covered with loose stones and flints after any spell of dry weather, the road goes hence steeply down into Winterborne Whitchurch, where the 'bourne,' from which the place takes the first half of its name, goes across the road in a hollow, and the church stands, with its neighbouring parsonage and cottages, in a lane running at right angles to the high-road, for all the world like Tarrant Hinton and Little Wallop. John Wesley, the grandfather of the founder of the 'Wesleyans'—or the 'Methodys,' as the country people call Methodists—was Vicar of Winterborne Whitchurch for a time during the Commonwealth; but as he seems never to have been regularly ordained, he was thrown out at the Restoration by 'malignants' and began a kind of John the Baptist life amid the hills and valleys of Dorsetshire, an exemplar for the imitation of his grandsons in later days. Itineracy and a sturdy independence thus became a tradition and a duty with the Wesleys. Thus are sects increased and multiplied, and no more sure way exists of producing prophets than by the persecution and oppression of those who, left judiciously alone, would live and die unknown to and unhonoured by the world.

Milborne St. Andrew, close upon three miles onward, is placed in another of these many deep hollows which, with streams running through them, are so recurrent a feature of the Exeter Road; only the hollow here is a broader one and better dignified with the title of valley. The stream of the 'mill-bourne,' from which the original mill has long since vanished (if, indeed, the name of the place is not, more correctly, 'Melbourne,' 'mell' in Dorsetshire meaning, like the prefix of 'lew' in Devon, a warm and sheltered spot), is a tributary of the river Piddle, which, a few miles down the road gives name to Piddletown, and along its course to Aff-Piddle, Piddletrenthide, Piddlehinton, Tolpiddle, and Turner's Piddle.

Milborne St. Andrew is a pretty place, and those who know Normandy may well think it, with its surrounding meads and feathery poplars, like a village in that old-world French province. Almost midway along the sixteen and a quarter miles between Blandford and Dorchester, it still keeps the look of an old coaching and posting village, although the last coach and the days of road-travel are beyond the recollection of the oldest inhabitant. Here, in the midst of the village, the street widens out, where the old 'White Hart,' now the Post Office, with a great effigy of a White Hart, and a number of miniature cannons on the porch roof, waits for the coaches that come no more, and for the dashing carriages and post-chaises that were driven away with their drivers and their gouty red-faced occupants to Hades, long, long ago. Is the 'White Hart,' standing like so many of these old hostelries beside the highway, waiting successfully for the revival of the roads, and will it live over the brave old days again with the coming of the Motor Car?

Meanwhile, given fine weather, there are few pleasanter places to spend a reminiscent afternoon in than Milborne St. Andrew.

The old church is up along the hillside, reached with the aid of a bye-road. Its tower, like that of Winterborne Whitchurch, shows the curious and rather pleasing local fashion of building followed four hundred years or so back, consisting of four to six courses of nobbled flints alternating with a course of ashlar. A stone in the east wall of the chancel to the memory of William Rice, servant to two of the local squires here for more than sixty years, ending in 1826, has the curious particulars:—

> He superintended the Harriers, and was the first Man who hunted a Pack of Roebuck Hounds.

At a point a mile and a half farther used to stand Dewlish turnpike gate, where the tolls were taken before coming down into Piddletown.

This large village is the 'Weatherbury' of some of Mr. Thomas Hardy's Wessex stories, and the Jacobean musicians' gallery of the fine unrestored church is vividly reminiscent of many humorous passages between the village choir in *Under the Greenwood Tree*. An organ stands there now, but the 'serpent,' the 'clar'net,' and the fiddles of Mr. Hardy's rustic choir would still seem more at home in that place.

Between this and Dorchester, past that end of Piddletown called 'Troy Town,' is Yellowham — one had almost written 'Yalbury' — Hill, crowned with the lovely woodlands described so beautifully under the name of 'Yalbury Woods' in that story, and drawn again in the opening scene of *Far from the Madding Crowd*, where Gabriel Oak, invisible in his leafy eyrie above the road, perceives Bathsheba's feminine vanities with the looking-glass.

Descending the western side of the hill and passing the broad park-lands of Kingston, we enter the town of Dorchester along the straight and level road running through the water-meadows of the river Frome. Until a few years ago this approach was shaded and rendered beautiful by an avenue of stately old elms that enclosed the distant picture of the town as in a frame; but they were cut down by the Duchy of Cornwall officials, in whose hands much of the surrounding property is placed, and only the pitiful stumps of them, shorn off close to the ground, remain to tell of their existence. As Dorchester is approached the road is seen in the distance becoming a street, and going, as straight as ever, and with a continuous rise,

WHITE HART

through the town, with the square tower of St. Peter's and the spiky clock-tower of the Town Hall cresting the view in High West Street, and in High East Street the modern Early English spire of All Saints nearer at hand. The particular one among the many bridges and culverts that carry the rivulets under the road here, mentioned by the novelist in his *Mayor of Casterbridge* as the spot where Henchard, the ruined mayor, lounged in his aimless idleness, amid the wastrels and ne'er-do-weels of Casterbridge, is the bridge that finally brings the road into the town, by the old 'White Hart Inn.' It is the inevitable lounging-stock for Dorchester's failures, who mostly live near by at Fordington, the east end of the town, where the 'Mixen Lane' of the story, 'the mildewed leaf in the sturdy and flourishing Casterbridge plant' was situated.

It is a transfigured Dorchester that is painted by the novelist in that story; or, perhaps more exactly, the Dorchester of fifty years ago. 'It is huddled all together; and it is shut in by a square wall of trees, like a plot of garden-ground by a box-edging,' is the not very apt comparison with the tall chestnuts and sycamores of the surviving avenues. 'It stood, with regard to the wide fertile land adjoining, clean-cut and distinct, like a chess-board on a green table-cloth. The farmer's boy could sit under his barley-mow and pitch a stone into the window of the town-clerk; reapers at work among the sheaves nodded to acquaintances standing on the pavement corner; the red-robed judge, when he condemned a sheep-stealer, pronounced sentence to the tune of Baa, that floated in at the window from the remainder of the flock browsing hard by.'

This peculiarity of Dorchester, a four-square clearly-defined *appliqué* of town upon a pastoral country, has been gradually disappearing during many years past, owing to an increase of population that has burst the ancient bounds imposed by the town being almost completely surrounded by the Duchy of Cornwall lands. This property, known by the name of Fordington Field (and not the existence at any time of a ford on the Frome), gives the eastern end of Dorchester its title. The land, let by the Duchy in olden times, in quarters or 'fourthings' of a carucate, gave the original name of 'Fourthington.' A great deal of this property has now been sold or leased for building purposes, and so the avenues that once clearly defined with their ramparts of greenery the bounds of Dorchester are now of a more urban character.

Dorchester shares with Blandford and with Marlborough a solid architectural character of a sober and responsible kind. As in those towns, imaginative Gothic gables and quaint mediaeval fancies are somewhat to seek amid the overwhelming proportion of Renaissance, or neo-classic, or merely Queen Anne and Georgian red-brick or stone houses. The cause of this may be sought in the recurrent disastrous fires that on four occasions practically swept the town out of existence, as in the case of Marlborough and Blandford. The earliest of these happened in 1613. Over three hundred houses were burnt on that occasion, and property amounting to nearly a quarter of a million sterling lost. This insistent scourge of the West of

England thatched houses visited the town again, nine years later, and also in 1725 and 1775. Little wonder, then, that mediæval Dorchester has to be sought for in nooks and corners. But if like those other unfortunate towns in these circumstances, it is very different in appearance, the streets being comparatively narrow and the houses of a more stolid and heavy character: so that only in sunny weather does Dorchester strike the stranger as being at all a cheerful place.

XXXVIII

All the incidents in Dorchester's history seem insignificant beside the tremendous melodrama of the 'Bloody Assize.' The stranger has eyes and ears for little else than the story of that terrible time, and longs to see the Court where Jeffreys sat, mad with drink and disease, and sentenced the unhappy prisoners to floggings, slavery, or death. Unhappily, that historic room has disappeared, but 'Judge Jeffreys' chair' is still to be seen in the modern Town Hall, and one can approach in imagination nearer to that awful year

JUDGE JEFFREYS' CHAIR.

of 1685 by gazing at 'Judge Jeffreys' Lodgings,' still standing in High West Street, over Dawes' china shop.

It must have been with a ferocious satisfaction that Jeffreys arrived here to open that Assize, for Dorchester had been a 'malignant' town and a thorn in the side of the Royalists forty years before. A kind of wild retribution was to fall upon it now, not only for the share that this district of the West had in Monmouth's Rebellion in this unhappy year, but for the Puritanism of a bygone generation.

Jeffreys reached here on 2nd September and the Assize was opened on the following day, lasting until the 8th. Macaulay has given a most convincing picture of it :—

'The Court was hung, by order of the Chief Justice, with scarlet; and this innovation seemed to the multitude to indicate a bloody purpose. It was also rumoured that when the clergyman, who preached the assize sermon, enforced the duty of mercy, the ferocious mouth of the Judge was distorted by an ominous grin. These things made men augur ill of what was to follow.

'More than three hundred prisoners were to be tried The work seemed heavy; but Jeffreys had a contrivance for making it light. He let it be understood that the only chance of obtaining pardon or respite was to plead guilty. Twenty-nine persons who put themselves on their country, and were convicted, were ordered to be tied up without delay. The remaining prisoners pleaded guilty by scores. Two hundred and ninety-two received sentence of death. The whole number hanged in Dorsetshire amounted to seventy-four.'

It is a relief to turn from such things to the less tragical coaching era. The 'King's Arms,' which was formerly the great coaching hostelry of Dorchester, still keeps pride of place here, and its capacious bay-windows of old-fashioned design yet look down upon the chief street. Instead, however, of the kings and princes and the great ones of the earth who used to be driven up in fine style in their 'chariots' a hundred years ago, and in place of the weary coach-travellers who used to alight at the hospitable doors of the 'King's Arms,' the commercial travellers of to-day are deposited here by the hotel omnibus from the railway station with little or no remains of that pomp and circumstance which accompanied arrivals in the olden time. King George the Third was well acquainted with this capacious house, for his horses were changed here on his numerous journeys through Dorchester between London, Windsor, and Weymouth. He kept a commonplace Court in the summer at Weymouth for many years, and thus made the fortune of that town, while his son, the Prince of Wales, was similarly making Brighthelmstone popular. If we are to believe the story of the Duchesse d'Abrantes, Napoleon had conceived the very theatrical idea of kidnapping the King on one of these journeys. The exploit was planned for execution in the wild and lonely country between Dorchester and Weymouth: possibly beneath the grim shadow of sullen Maumbury, or of prehistoric Maiden Castle. The King and his escort were to have been surprised by a party of secretly-landed French sailors, and his Majesty forthwith hustled on board an open boat which was then to be rowed across the Channel to Cherbourg. According to this remarkable statement, the English coastguards had been heavily bribed to assist in this affair. It was magnificent, but it was not war—nor even business. As an elaborate joke, the project has its distinctly humorous aspects, as one vividly conjures up a picture of 'Farmer George,' helplessly sea-sick, leaning on the gunwale of the row-boat, with the equally unhappy sailors toiling away at rowing those seventy miles of salt water. Then, too, the thought of that essentially unromantic King compelled to cut a ridiculous figure as a kind of modern travesty of the imprisoned Richard Lionheart, raises a smile. But, although Napoleon, who was not a gentleman, may very possibly have entertained this rather characteristic notion, he certainly never attempted to put it into execution, and the road to Weymouth is by so much the poorer in incident.

But to return to the 'King's Arms,' which figures in Mr. Thomas Hardy's story. Here it was, looking in with the crowd on the street, that Susan saw her long-lost husband presiding as Mayor at the banquet, the beginning of all his troubles.

Although the stranger who has no ties with Dorchester to help paint it in such glowing colours as those used by that writer, who finds it 'one of the cleanest and prettiest towns in the West of England,' cannot subscribe to that description, the town is of a supreme interest to the literary pilgrim, who can identify many spots hallowed by Mr. Hardy's genius.

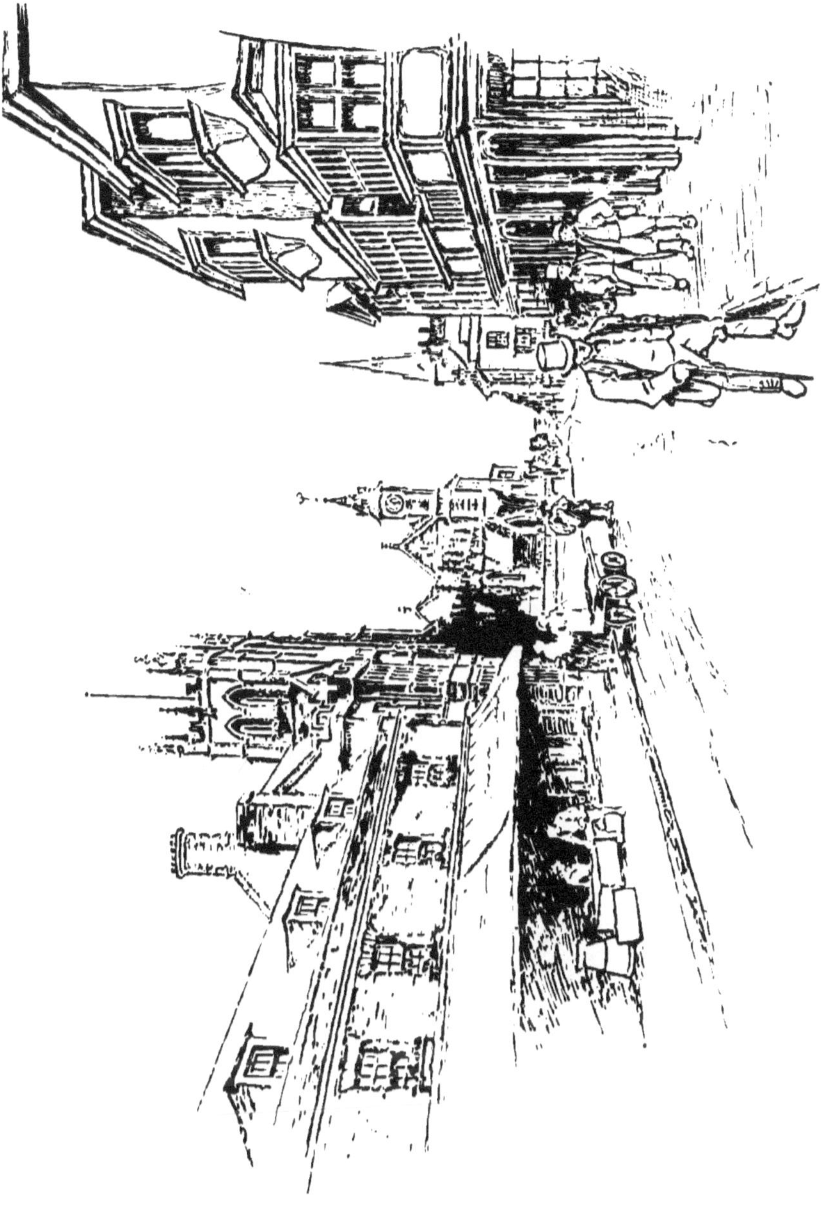

There are those in Dorsetshire who bitterly resent the Tony Kytes, the Car Darches, the Bathshebas, and in especial poor Tess, who flit through his unconventional pages, and hold that he deprives the Dorset peasant of his moral character; but if you hold no brief for the natives in their relation to the Ten Commandments, why, it need matter little or nothing to you whether his characters are intended as portraitures, or are evolved wholly from a peculiar imagination. It remains only to say that they are very real characters to the reader, who can follow their loves and hatreds, their comedy and tragedy, and can trace their footsteps with a great deal more personal interest than can be stirred up over the doings of many historical personages.

XXXIX

The Exeter Road begins to rise immediately on leaving Dorchester. Leaving the town by a fine avenue of ancient elms stretching for half a mile, the highway runs, with all the directness characteristic of a Roman road, on a gradual incline up the bare and open expanse of Bradford Down, unsheltered as yet by the stripling trees newly planted as a continuation of the dense avenue just left behind. The first four miles of road from the town are identical with the Roman *Via Iceniana*, the Icen Way or Icknield Street; and on the left rises, at the distance of a mile away, the sombre Roman earthwork of Maiden

Castle crowning a hill forming with the earthen amphitheatre of Poundbury on the right hand, evidence, if all else in Dorchester were wanting, of the importance of the place at that remote period.

At the fourth milestone the Exeter Road leaves that ancient military way, and, turning sharply to the left, goes down steeply, amid loose gravel and rain-runnels, to Winterborne Abbas, with an exceedingly awkward fork to the road to Weymouth on the left hand half-way down. Bold and striking views of the sullen ridge of Blackdown, with Admiral Hardy's pillar on the ridge, are unfolded as one descends.

XL.

Winterborne Abbas, one of the twenty-five Winterbornes that plentifully dot the map of Wilts and Dorset, lies on the level at the bottom of this treacherous descent: a small village of thatched cottages with a church too large for it, overhung by fir trees, and a remodelled old coaching inn, apparently also too large, with its sign swinging picturesquely from a tree-trunk on the opposite side of the road which, like the majority of Dorsetshire roads, is rich in loose flints.

Half a mile beyond the village, a railed enclosure on the strip of grass on the left-hand side of the road attracts the wayfarer's notice. This serves to protect from the attentions of the stone-breaker a group of eight prehistoric stones called the 'Broad Stone.'

WINTERBORNE ABBAS.

The largest is 10 feet long by 5 feet, and 2 feet thick, lying down. A notice informs all who care to know that this group is constituted by the owner, according to the Act of Parliament, an 'Ancient Monument.' The cynically-minded might well say that the hundreds of similar 'ancient monuments' with which the neighbouring downs are peppered might also be railed off, to give a welcome fillip to the trade in iron fencing, and certainly this caretaking of every misshapen stone without a story is the New Idolatry.

Just beyond this point is the castellated lodge of the park of Bridehead, embowered amid trees. The place obtains its name from the little river Bride or Bredy which rises in the grounds and flows away to enter the sea at Burton (= 'Bride-town') Bradstock, eight miles away; passing in its course the two other places named from it, Little Bredy and Long Bredy.

Now the road rises again, and ascends wild unenclosed downs which gradually assume a stern, and even mountainous, character. Amid this panorama, in the deep hollows below these stone-strewn heights, are gracious wooded dells, doubly beautiful by contrast. In the still and sheltered nooks of these sequestered spots the primrose blooms early, and frosts come seldom, while the uplands are covered with snow or swept with bleak winds that freeze the traveller's very marrow. One of these gardens in the wilderness is Kingston Russell, the spot whence the Russells, now Dukes of Bedford, sprang from obscurity into wealth and power. Deep down in their retirement, the world (or such small proportion of it as travelled in those days) passed unobserved, though not far removed. For generations the Russells had inhabited their old manor-house here, and might have done so, in undistinguished fashion, for many years more, had it not been for the chance which brought John Russell into prominence and preferment in 1502. He was the Founder of the House and died an Earl, with vast estates, the spoil of the Church, showered upon him. He was the first of all

KINGSTON RUSSELL.

the Russells to exhibit that gift of 'getting on' which his descendants have almost uniformly inherited. Unlike him, however, they have rarely commanded affection, and the Dukes of Bedford, with much reason, figure in the public eye as paragons of meanness and parsimony.

At the cross roads, where on the left the bye-path leads steeply down the sides of these immemorial hills to Long Bredy, and on the right in the direction of Maiden Newton, used to stand Long Bredy Gate and the 'Hut Inn.' Here the high-road is continued along the very backbone of the ridge, exposed to all the rigours of the elements. To add to the weird aspect of the scene, barrows and tumuli are scattered about in profusion. We now come to a turning on the left hand called 'Cuckold's Corner,' why, no legend survives to tell us. Steeply this lane leads to the downs that roll away boldly to the sea, coming in

CHILCOMBE CHURCH.

little over a mile to 'chilly Chilcombe,' a tiny hamlet with a correspondingly tiny church tucked away among the great rounded shoulders of the hills, but not so securely sheltered but that the eager winds find their way to it and render both name and epithet eminently descriptive. The population of Chilcombe, according to the latest census, is twenty-four, and the houses six; and it is, accordingly, quite in order that the church should be regarded as the smallest in England. There are many of these 'smallest churches,' and the question as to which really deserves the title is not likely to be determined until an expedition is fitted out to visit all these rival claimants, and to accurately measure them. Of course the remaining portions of a church are not eligible for inclusion in this category. Chilcombe, however, is a complete example. The hamlet was never, in all probability, more populous than it is now, and the church certainly was never larger. Originally Norman, it underwent some alterations in the late Perpendicular period. The measurements are: nave 22 feet in length, chancel 13 feet. It is a picturesque though unassuming little building, without a tower, but provided instead with a quaint old stone bell-cote on the west gable. This gives the old church the appearance of some ancient ecclesiastical pigeon-house. The bell within is dated 1656. The very fine and unusual altar-piece of dark walnut wood, with scenes from the life of Christ, is credibly reported to have been brought here from one of the ships of the 'Invincible Armada,' known to have been wrecked on the beach at Burton Bradstock, some three miles away.

Returning to the highway at 'Cuckold's Corner,' we come to 'Traveller's Rest,' now a wayside inn on the left hand, situated on the tremendous descent which commences a mile beyond Long Bredy turnpike, and goes practically down into Bridport's long street; a distance of five miles, with a fall from 702 feet above the sea, to 253 feet at 'Traveller's Rest,' two miles farther on, and eventually to sea-level at

Bridport, with several curves in the road and an intermediate ascent or two between this point and the town. The cyclist who cares to take his courage in both hands, and has no desire to linger over perhaps one of the most magnificent scenic panoramas in England, can coast down this long stretch with the speed of the wind, and chance the result. But it is better to loiter here, for none of the great high-roads has anything like this scenery to show. From away up the road the eye ranges over a vast stretch of country westwards. South-west lies the Channel, dazzling like a burnished mirror if you come here at the psychological moment for this view—that is to say, the late afternoon of a summer's day; with the strangely contorted shapes of the hills round about suggesting volcanic origin, and casting cool shadows far down into the sheltered coombes that have been baking in the sun all day long. Near at hand is Shipton Beacon, rising almost immediately beyond 'Traveller's Rest,' and looking oddly from some points of view like some gigantic ship's hull lying keel uppermost. Beyond are Puncknoll and Hammerdon, and away in the distance, with the Channel sparkling behind it, and the sun making a halo for its head, overlooking the sea at a height of 615 feet, the grand crest of Golden Cap, which some hold to be so named from this circumstance, while others have it that the picturesque title derives from the yellow gorse that grows on its summit. To the right hand rises the natural rampart of Eggardon, additionally fortified by art, a thousand years ago, whether by Briton, Dane, or Saxon, let those determine who will, with the village of Askerswell lying deep down, immediately under this ridge on which the road goes, the roof of its village church tower apparently so near that you could drop a stone neatly on to its leads. But 'one trial will suffice,' as the advertisements of much-puffed articles say, for the stone goes no nearer than about a quarter of a mile.

Very charming, this panorama, on a summer's day; but how about the winters' nights, in the times when the 'Traveller's Rest' was better named than now; when the coaches halted here, and coachmen, guards, and passengers alike, half-frozen and breathless from the blusterous heights of Long Bredy, tumbled out for something warming? For this hillside was reputed to be the coldest part of the journey between London and Exeter, and it may be readily enough supposed by all who have seen the spot, that this was indeed the fact.

XLI

The last mile into Bridport has none of these terrify-descents, although, to be sure, there are sudden curves in the road which it behoves the cyclist to take slowly, for they may develop anything in the way of traffic, from a traction engine to the elephantine advance-guard of a travelling circus.

At Bridport, nine miles from the Devon border, the country already begins to lose something of the Dorset character, and to look like the county of junket and clotted cream. As for the town, it is difficult to say what character it possesses, for its featureless High Street is redeemed only from tediousness by the belfry of the Town Hall which, with the fine westward view, including the conical height of Colmer's Hill and the high table-land of Eype to the left, serves to compose the whole into something remotely resembling an effect.

Bridport is a town which would very much like to be on the sea, but is, as a matter of fact, situated rather over a mile from it. Just where the little river Bredy runs out and the sea comes banging furiously in, is a forlorn concourse of houses sheltering abjectly one behind the other, called variously Bridport Harbour and West Bay. This is the real port, but it matters little, or nothing at all, by what name you call the place; it remains more like a Port Desolation.

Bridport almost distinguished itself in 1651 by the fugitive Charles the Second having been nearly captured at the 'George Inn' by the Harbour, an ostler recognising his face, which, it must be conceded, was one that once seen could scarce have been mistaken when again met with. Charles was then trying to reach the coast after the disastrous battle of Worcester, and it is quite certain that if Cromwell's troopers had laid their hands on him, there would never have been any Charles the Second in English history.

The tragical comedy of the Stuarts throws a glamour over the Exeter Road to its very end. The fugitive Charles, fleeing before the inquisitive stare of the ostler, is a striking picture; and so, thirty-four years later, is the coming of his partly acknowledged son, the Duke of Monmouth, to upset James the

Second. Bridport was seized, and one of the 'Monmouth men' slew Edward Coker, gentleman, of Mappowder, on the 14th of June 1685, as the memorial tablet to that slaughtered worthy in Bridport parish church duly recounts. For their share in the rebellion, a round dozen of Bridport men were hanged before the eyes of their neighbours, 'stabbed,' as the ancient slang phrase has it, 'with a Bridport dagger.' The ghastly imagery of this saying derives from the old-time local manufacture of rope, twine, and string, and the cultivation of hemp in the surrounding country. Rope- and twine-walks still remain in the town.

Leaving Bridport behind, the coach passengers by this route presently came to its most wildly romantic part; only it is sad to reflect that the travellers of a hundred years ago had not the slightest appreciation of this kind of thing.

> Through Bridport's stony lanes our way we take,
> And the proud steep descend to Morcombe's lake.

Thus the poet Gay, but he writes from the horseman's point of view, and if he had bruised his bones along this road in the lurching Exeter Fly, his tone would probably have been less breezy. Travellers, indeed, looked upon hills with loathing, and upon solitude (notwithstanding the poets of the time) with disgust: therefore it may well be supposed that when they came to the rugged scenery around Morecomb-lake, and the next village Chideock (called locally 'Chiddick'), they did not enjoy themselves.

Here Stonebarrow Hill and Golden Cap, with many

lesser eminences, frown down upon the steep highway on every side, and render the scenery nothing less than mountainous, so that strangers in these parts, overcome with 'terrour' and apprehensions of worse to come, wished themselves safe housed in the roadside inn of Morecomblake, whose hospitable sign gave, and still gives, promise of good entertainment.

The run down into Charmouth from this point is

CHIDEOCK

a breakneck one. At this remote seaside place, in that same year, 1651, Charles the Second had another narrow escape. Travelling in bye-ways from the disastrous field of Worcester on horseback, with his staunch friends, Lord Wilmot and Colonel Wyndham, arrangements had been made with the master of a trading vessel hailing from Lyme, to put in at Charmouth with a boat in the stillness of the night. But they had reckoned without taking into account either the simplicity of the sailor, or the inquisitiveness of his wife, who wormed the secret out of him, of his being engaged in this mysterious affair with a party of strangers. All the country was ringing with the escape of Charles from Worcester and the hue and cry after him, and the woman rightly guessed whom these people might be. She effectually prevented her husband from putting in an appearance by the threat

SIGN OF THE 'SHIP,' MORECOMBLAKE.

that if he made any such attempt she would inform the magistrate.

Wearied with watching for the promised boat, the King's companions reluctantly had to make Charmouth the resting-place of the party for the night. In the morning it was found that the King's horse had cast a shoe. When it was taken to the blacksmith, that worthy remarked the quaint circumstance that the three others had been replaced in three different counties, and one of these three in Worcestershire.

When Charles heard that awkward discovery he was off in haste, for if a rural blacksmith was clever enough to discover so much, it was quite possible that he might apply his knowledge in a very embarrassing manner.

The little band had not hurried away a moment too soon, for the ostler of the inn (what Sherlock Holmes's all these Dorsetshire folks were, to be sure!) who had already arrived independently at the conclusion that this was King Charles, had in the meanwhile gone to the Rev. Bartholomew Wesley, a local Roundhead divine, and told him his thoughts. Thence to the inn, where legends tell us the landlady gave Mr. Wesley a fine full-flavoured piece of her mind, and so eventually to the ears of a captain of horse, this wondrous news spread. Horsemen scoured the country: clergyman returned home to think over the loyal landlady's abuse: ostler, probably dismissed, had leisure to curse his officiousness; while King and companions were off, whip and spur, to Bridport, whence, after that alarming recognition at the Harbour, to Broadwinsor.

INTERIOR OF THE 'QUEEN'S ARMS,' CHARMOUTH

This historic Charmouth inn is still existing. The 'Anchor,' as it is now known, was for many years the 'Queen's Arms,' but although the sign has thus been altered and half of the building partitioned off as a separate house, the interior remains very much the same as it was then, and the original rough, stone-flagged passages, dark panelling, and deep-embrasured windows add a convincing touch to the story of the King's flight through England with a price on his head.

For the rest, Charmouth, which stands where the tiny river Char empties itself into the sea, consists of one long street of mutually antagonistic houses, of all shapes, sizes, and materials, and is the very exemplar of a fishing village turned into an inchoate seaside resort. But a sunny, sheltered, and pleasing spot.

On leaving Charmouth, the road begins to ascend again, and leaves Dorsetshire for Devon through a tunnel cut in the hillside, called the 'New Passage,' coming in four miles to 'Hunter's Lodge Inn,' picturesquely set amid a forest of pine trees. From this point it is two and a half miles on to Axminster, a town which still gives a name to a particular make of carpets, although since 1835 the local factories have been closed and the industry transferred to Wilton, in Wiltshire. It was in 1755 that the industry was started here.

There is one fine old coaching inn, the 'George,' at Axminster, with huge rambling stables and interminable corridors, in which one ought to meet the ghosts of departed travellers on the Exeter Road. But they are shy. There should, in fact, be many ghosts in this old town of many memories; and so there are, to that clairvoyant optic, the 'mind's eye.' But they refuse to materialise to the physical organ, and it is only to a vivid imagination that the streets are repeopled with the excited peasantry who, in that fatal summer of 1685, flocked to the standard of the Duke of Monmouth, whom 'the Lord raised vp' as the still existing manuscript narrative of an Axminster dissenting minister says, to champion the Protestant religion—with what results we already know.

Pleasant meadow-lands lead by flat and shaded roads from Axminster by the river Axe to Axmouth, Seaton, and the sea, but our way continues inland.

XLII

There are steep ups and downs on the nine miles and a half between Axminster, the byegone home of carpets, and Honiton, once the seat of the lace industry, where all routes from London to Exeter meet. 'Honiton lace' is made now in the surrounding villages, but not in the town itself.

The first hill is soon met with, on passing over the river Yart. This is Shute Hill, where the coaches generally were upset, if either the coachman or the horses were at all 'fresh.' Then it is a long run down to Kilmington, where the travellers, having recovered their hearts from their boots or their throats, according to their temperaments, and found their breath, promptly cursed those coachmen and threatened them with all manner of pains and penalties for reckless driving. Thence, by way of Wilmington, to Honiton.

A quarter of a mile before reaching that town the traveller comes upon a singular debased Gothic toll-house. If he walks or cycles he may pass freely, but all carts and cattle have still to pay toll. This queer survival is known as King's Road Gate, or by the more popular name of 'Copper Castle,' from its once having a peaked copper roof above its carpenter-gothic battlements.

'COPPER CASTLE.'

Honiton, whose name is locally 'Honeyton,' is a singularly uninteresting town, with its mother-parish church half a mile away from the one broad street that forms practically the whole of the place. Clean, quiet, and neither very old nor very new, so far as outward appearance goes, Honiton must be of a positively deadly dulness to the tourist on a rainy day; when to go out of doors is to get wet, and to remain in, thrown on the slender resources for amusement afforded by the local papers and the ten-years-old county directory in the hotel coffee-room, is a weariness.

Once a year, during Honiton Great Fair, this long, empty street is not too wide; but all the year round, and every year, the broad highway hence on to Exeter is a world too spacious for its shrunken traffic. Broad selvedges of grass encroach as slyly as a land-grabbing, enclosing country gentleman upon this generous width of macadamised surface, and are allowed their will of all but a narrow strip sufficient for the present needs of the traffic. It is fifty-five years since the Great Western Railway was opened through to Exeter, and during that more than half a century these long reaches of the road have been deserted. Do belated cyclists, wheeling on moonlit nights along this tree-shaded road, ever conjure up a picture of the last mail down: the farewells at the inns, the cottagers standing at their doors, or leaning out of their windows, to see the visible passing away of an epoch; the flashing of the lamps past the hedgerows, and the last faint echoes of the horn sounding in melancholy fashion a mile away? If they do not, why then they must be sadly lacking in imagination, or ill-read in the Story of the Roads.

Where the roads branch in puzzling fashion, four and a half miles from Honiton, and all ways seem to lead to Exeter, there stands on the grassy plot at the fork a roadside monument to a missionary bishop, Dr. Patteson, who, born 1st April 1827, met martyrdom, together with two other workers in the mission-field, in New Zealand, in 1871. He was the eldest son of Sir John Patteson, of Feniton Court, near by, hence the placing of this brick and stone column here, surmounted by a cross, and plentifully inscribed with texts. The story of his and his friends' death is set forth as having been 'in vengeance for wrongs suffered at the hands of Europeans by savage men whom he loved and for whose sake he gave up home and country and friends dearer than his life.'

This memorial also serves the turn of finger-post, for directions are carved on its four sides; and very necessary too, for where two roads go to Exeter, the one by Ottery St. Mary some two miles longer than the other, the passing rustic is not wholly to be depended upon for clear and concise information. Cobbett in his day found that exasperating direction of the rustics to the inquiring wayfarer, to 'keep straight on,' just as great a delusion as the tourist now discovers it to be. The formula, according to him, was a little different in his time, being 'keep *right* on.'

'Aye,' says he, 'but in ten minutes, perhaps, you come to a Y or a T, or to a X. A fellow once told me, in my way from Chertsey to Guildford, "keep *right on*, you can't miss your way." I was in the perpendicular part of the T, and the top part was only a few yards from me. "*Right on*," said I, "what, over *that bank* into the wheat?"—"No, no," said he, "I mean *that road*, to be sure," pointing to the road that went off to the *left*.'

Here a branch of the river Otter crosses the road in the wooded dell of Fenny Bridges, and in the course of another mile, on the banks of another stream, stands the 'Fair Mile Inn,' the last stage into

Exeter in coaching times. Lonely the road remains, passing the scattered cottages of Rockbeare, and the depressing outlying houses of Honiton Clyst, situated on the little river Clyst, with the first of the characteristic old red sandstone church-towers of the South Devon looking down upon the road from the midst of embowering foliage. Then the squalid east end of Exeter and the long street of Heavitree, where Exeter burnt her martyrs, come into view, and there, away in front, with its skyline of towers and spires, is Exeter, displayed in profile for the admiration of all who have journeyed these many miles to where she sits in regal grandeur upon her hill that descends until its feet are bathed in the waters of her godmother, the Exe. Her streets are steep and her site dignified, although it is partly the level range of the surrounding country, rather than an intrinsic height, which confers that look of majesty which all travellers have noticed. The ancient city rises impressive in contrast with the water-meadows, rather than by reason of actual measurement. Wayfarers approaching from any direction brace themselves and draw deep breaths preparatory to scaling the streets, which, at a distance, assume abrupt vistas. Villas, with spacious gardens, and snug, prebendal-looking houses, eloquent of a thousand a year and cellars full of old port, clothe the lower slopes of this rising ground, to give place, by degrees, to streets which, as the traveller advances, grow narrower and more crooked, their lines of houses becoming ever older, more picturesque, and loftier as they near the heart of the city. Modernity inhabits the environs, antiquity is seated, impressive, in the centre, where, on a plateau, closely hemmed in from the bustling, secular life of the streets, rises the sombre mass of the cathedral, the pride of this western land.

XLIII

Exeter is called by those who know her best and love her most the 'Queen City of the West.' To historians she is perhaps better epithetically remembranced as the 'Ever Faithful,' loyal and staunch through the good fortune or adversity of the causes for which she has, with closed and guarded gates, held fast the Key of the West. She has suffered much at different periods of her history for this loyalty; from the time when, declaring against the usurpation of Stephen, her citizens fought and starved within the walls; through the centuries to the time of Perkin Warbeck, the impostor, and so on to the Civil War between King and Parliament, when the citizens were more loyal than their rulers and were disarmed and kept under surveillance until the Royalists came and took the place, themselves to be dispossessed a few years later.

Loyalty, tried for so many centuries at so great a cost, broke down finally in 1688, and the city gates were opened to the Prince of Orange. Had James been less of a bigot, and had his hell-hounds, Jeffreys and Kirke, been animated with less zeal, who knows what these Devonshire men would have done? Possibly it may be said that William's fleet would, under such circumstances, never have found its way into Tor Bay, nor that historic landing have been consummated at Brixham. True enough; but granting the landing, the proclamation at Newton Abbot, and the advance to the gates of Exeter, how then if James had been less of the stubborn oak and more of the complaisant willow? Can it be supposed that they would have welcomed this frigid, hawk-nosed foreigner of the cold eye and silent tongue? And if the Dutchman and his mynheers had been ill-received at Exeter, what then? Take the map and study it for answer. You will see that the 'Ever Faithful' stands at the Gates of the West. The traveller always has had to enter these portals if he would go in either direction, and the more imperative was this necessity to those coming from West to East. Even now the traveller by railway passes through Exeter to reach further Devon and Cornwall, equally with him who fares the high-road.

What chance, then, of success would a foreign expedition command were its progress barred at this point? Less mobile than a single traveller, or party of mere travellers, it could not well evade the struggle for a passage by taking another route. William and his following might, in such an event, have at great risk forced the passage of the treacherous Exe estuary, but even supposing that feat achieved, there is difficult country beyond, before the road to London is reached. To the northwards of his march from Brixham lies Dartmoor and its outlying hills, and let those who have explored those inhospitable wastes weigh the chances of a force marching through the hostile countryside in the depth of winter to outflank Exeter.

But all hope for James's cause was gone, and although the spirits of the ambitious William sank when, on entering the streets of Exeter, he was only received with a chilly curiosity, he was not to know —for how could that most stony of champions read into the hearts of these people?—that their generous enthusiasm for faith and freedom was quite crushed out of existence by the bloody work of three years before, when the peasantry saw with horror the progress of the fiendish Jeffreys marked by a line of gibbets; when they could not fare forth upon the highways and byeways without presently arriving at some Golgotha rubricated with the dishonoured remains of one or other of their fellows; and when many a cottage had its empty chair, the occupants dead or sold into a slavery worse than death.

The people received William with a well-simulated lack of interest, because they knew what would be their portion were he defeated and James again triumphant. They could not have cherished any personal affection for the Prince of Orange, but can only, at the best of it, have had an impersonal regard for him as a champion of their liberties; and of helping such champions they had already acquired a bitter surfeit. Thus it was that the back of loyalty was broken, and Exeter, for once in her story, belied her motto, *Semper Fidelis*, the gift of Queen Elizabeth.

The gifts that loyalty has brought Exeter may soon be enumerated, for they comprise just a number of charters conferred by a long line of sovereigns; an Elizabethan motto; a portrait of his sister, presented by Charles the Second; a Sword of Honour, and an old hat, the gifts of Henry the Seventh in recognition of Exeter's stand against Perkin Warbeck in 1497. Against these parchments, this picture, and the miscellaneous items of motto, sword, and old hat, there are centuries of fighting and of spoliation on account of loyalty to be named. It seems a very one-sided affair, even though the old hat be a Cap of Maintenance and heraldically notable. Among the maces and the loving-cups, and all the civic regalia of Exeter, these objects are yet to be seen. Old headgear will wear out, and so the Cap, in its present form, dates back only to the time of James the First. It is by no means a gossamer, weighing, as it does, seven pounds. As may be seen by the accompanying illustration, it is a broad-brimmer of the most pronounced type.

THE EXETER CITY SWORD-BEARER

The crown fixed upon the point of the sword-sheath belongs to the same period, while a guinea of the same reign may be seen let into the metal of the pommel. On occasions of State, at Exeter, this sword is carried before the Mayor and Corporation by their official Sword-Bearer.

The dignified effect of the affair, however, is

generally spoiled by the commonplace black kid gloves worn by him, and by his everyday clothes visible under the official robes, which can be seen in the illustration.

Of late the Cap has been replaced by one built on the lines of those worn by the Yeomen of the Guard in the Tower of London, the old Cap being thought too historical to be any longer exposed to the danger of being worn, while possibly some feelings of humanity towards the Sword-Bearer may have dictated the replacing of the seven-pound hat by something lighter. It is now preserved in the Guildhall, where it may be seen by curious visitors.

XLIV

It is a relief to turn from the thronging streets to the absolute quiet of the cathedral precincts, shaded by tall elms and green with trim lawns.

Externally, the cathedral is of the grimiest and sootiest aspect—black as your hat, but comely. Not even the blackest corners of St. Paul's Cathedral, in London, show a deeper hue than the west front of St. Peter's, at Exeter. The battered, time-worn array of effigies of saints, kings, crusaders, and bishops that range along the screen in mutilated array under Bishop Grandison's great west window are black, too, and so are the gargoyles that leer with stony grimaces down upon you from the ridges and string-courses of the transepts, where they lurk in an enduring crepuscule.

The sonorous note of Great Peter, the great bell of the cathedral, sounding from the south transept tower is in admirable keeping with the black-browed gravity of the close, and keeps the gaiety of the surrounding hotels within the limits of a canonical sobriety.

Elsewhere are ancient hostelries innumerable, with yawning archways under which the coaches entered in the byegone days. The 'Elephant,' the 'Mermaid,' and the 'Half Moon' are the chief among these, and have the true Pickwickian air, which is the outstanding note of all inns of the Augustan age of coaching. It must have been worth the journey to be so worthily housed at the end of the alarums and excursions which more or less cheerfully enlivened the way.

Exeter and the far West of England were the last strongholds of the coaching interest. The Great Western Railway was opened to Exeter on 1st May 1844, and up to that time over seventy coaches left that city daily for London and the cross-country routes. Nor did coaching languish towards the close. On the contrary, it died game, and, until finally extinguished by the opening of the railway, coaching on the old road between London and Exeter was a matter of the utmost science and the best speed ever attained by the aid of four horses on a turnpike road. Charles Ward, the best-known driver of the old 'Telegraph' Exeter coach, driven from his old route, retreated westwards and took the road between Exeter and Devonport, retiring into Cornwall when the railway was opened to Plymouth on 1st May

1848; but not before he had brought the time of the 'Telegraph' between London and Exeter down to fifteen hours.

The 'Half Moon' is the inn from which the 'Telegraph' started at 6.30 in the morning, breakfasting at Ilminster, dining at Andover, and stopping for no other meal, reaching Hyde Park Corner at 9.30 P.M. It was kept in 1777 by a landlord named Hemming, who had a very good understanding with the highwaymen Boulter and Caldwell, and doubtless with many another. There is a record of those two knights of the road being here, one of them with a stolen horse, when a Mr. Harding, of Bristol, being in the yard, recognised it. 'Why, Mr. Hemming,' said he, 'that is the very mare my father-in-law, Mr. James, lost a few months ago; how came she here?' To which the landlord replied, 'She has been my own mare these twelve months, and how should she be your father-in-law's?'

'Well,' replied Harding, 'if I had seen her in any other hands, or met her on the road, I could have sworn to her.' Boulter and Caldwell were at that moment in the house at dinner, so the landlord took the first opportunity of warning them.

For the rest, Exeter is still picturesque. It possesses many quaint and interesting churches, placed in the strangest positions; while that of St. Mary Steps has a queer old clock with grotesque figures that strike the hours and chime the quarters. The seated figure is intended to represent Henry the Eighth, and those on either side of him men-at-arms, but the local people have a rhyming legend which

would have it that the King is a certain 'Matty the Miller':—

> The people around would not believe
> That Matty the Miller was dead;
> For every hour on Westgate tower,
> Matty still nods his head.

And, in fact, the King kicks his heels against the bell and nods with every stroke. The Jacobean Guildhall of Exeter, too, is among the most striking relics of this old-world city; while away from the High Street, but near the continual clashing of a great railway station, there stand the remains of Exeter Castle, the appropriately named Rougemont, that cruel Blunderbore, drunken in the long ago with the blood of many a gallant gentleman. At the end of a long line of those who suffered were Colonel John Penruddocke and Hugh Grove, captured at South Molton after that ineffectual Salisbury rising. Executed in the Castle Yard, in the very heart of this loyal city of Exeter, many a heart must have ached on that fatal morning for these unhappy men. 'This, I hope,' said Penruddocke, ascending the scaffold, 'will prove like Jacob's Ladder; though the feet of it rest upon the earth, yet I doubt not but the top of it reaches to Heaven. The crime for which I am now to die is Loyalty, in this age called High Treason.'

'MATTY THE MILLER.'

They knew both how to fight and how to die, those dauntless Cavaliers. The Earl of Derby, who suffered at Bolton, Sir Charles Lucas and Sir George Lisle, barbarously shot at the taking of Colchester; gray-haired Sir Nicholas Kemys at Chepstow, and many another died as valiantly as their master—

> Who nothing little did, nor mean,
> But bowed his shapely head
> Down, as upon a bed.

It is away through the city and across the Exe, to where the road rises in the direction of Dartmoor, that one of the finest views back upon the streets and the cathedral is obtained. Exeter from the Dunsford road, glimpsed by the ancient and decrepit elm pictured here, is worth seeing and the view itself is worth preserving, for elm and old-world foreground, with the inevitable changes which the growth of Exeter is bringing about, will not long remain. Like many another relic of a past era along this old highway, they are vanishing even while the busy chronicler of byegone days is hastening to record them.

INDEX

www.ingramcontent.com/pod-product-compliance
Lightning Source LLC
Chambersburg PA
CBHW020942030726
47496CB00005B/1316
9783744777667